Praise for *Care Under Fire*

Bill Strusinski had an uneventful upbringing. He was brought up to respect God, the Flag and our everyday institutions. He was a good student and had the makings to be a solid citizen. Vietnam pushed him into a highly elite (and small minority) group of people that were called on the do what few others could. He was a combat soldier. After his brief Army training in combat technique and ten weeks of medic training, he was called on to serve one year of constant combat. He performed surgery, psychological counseling, and all types of medical treatment to the soldiers with whom he served. He was constantly shot at and returned fire while saving lives of colleagues. He did things doctors with over eight years of training would have trouble doing. He saved lives and he still mourns the soldiers who died in his arms because he could not save them. He treated enemy POW's and civilian non-combatants who were injured in the horrors that were faced in Vietnam.

Several million Americans wore the uniform of the United States during the Vietnam years. But a small minority were ground combat soldiers engaged in ground combat. Bill's book is remarkable in telling the story of average young people who our country called on to fight for us. His talking about everyday problems of soldiers will bring back to our heroes who did the fighting the problems they faced and the pride they felt in serving honorably. The way Sergeant Strusinski tells the stories will remind his fellow heroes that their cause was just and that they did their duty. He does not dwell on the reception at home when he went from the jungle to civilization in America, but his recollections remind all of us the dishonorable way our heroes were treated when they returned to America.

Bill Strusinski did his duty and then went on to be the kind of citizen we wish we had more of in our country. He is not asking for thanks or anything else except, after 50 years, the chance to tell this remarkable story. We owe him, and his combat colleagues our thanks, our apology, and our respect. The hundreds of us who have known him in the fifty years since he became a civilian have known that he is an exceptional man. Now we know what he has been through. Our respect for him was high before we knew his story. Now we continue to respect and enjoy him on a whole new level. Everyone who respects America and what we stand for will benefit from this book and will get an understanding of the warriors who have made our country great.

Harry Sieben, Jr., Brigadier General, US Air Force, Retired

Bill Strusinski's *Care Under Fire* is a must read for military, combat medics, EMTs and all first responders! This is the self-help book for those of us that have served in the military or as first responders and have had to deal with PTSD, the haunting questions and guilt when we lose soldier or patient… "what did I forget to do" or "could I have done more".

This book describes the transformation of Strusinski from a self-doubting, out of shape college drop-out into a confident, physically fit, combat soldier. He describes the plane ride over, not knowing what to expect, the heat and smells when the plane lands and being the "new guy" that must prove himself worthy. It describes the hardships of Vietnam, combat, returning home and the new normal.

Bill Strusinski not only proved himself worthy, he is a true American hero as both his military awards and civilian life attest to. Anyone that has served knows that to earn a Valor Award is putting others above one's self but to earn three Bronze Stars with Valor not only tells a great deal about a person, it sets them apart. Bill Strusinski will tell you he just did his job and it is a job that many "Docs" do every day. Sometimes it is just being in the wrong place at the right time, I can agree with that but Doc Strusinski was there many times during his leap year in Vietnam. This book is about his story and how he was able to deal with the weight of the job, and all of us can learn from that.

This book is a great read and I believe it tells the legacy of an American Soldier.

Jeff Howe, Lieutenant Colonel, Minnesota Army National Guard, Retired

In a few pages, Bill Strusinski has captured in vivid detail the trepidation and fears of a young soldier in Vietnam who managed to balance the inconsistences and horror of war with instinctive bravery as he gave his heart and soul to his wounded comrades, eventually coming out of it all with a high degree of post traumatic strength.

Jerry Newton, Command Sergeant Major, US Army, Retired

Support our veterans!

Bill "Doc" Strusinski

Care Under Fire

Bill Strusinski

Wisdom
Editions
Minneapolis

Wisdom
Editions

Minneapolis

First Edition April 2020
CARE UNDER FIRE. Copyright © 2020 by Bill Strusinski.
All rights reserved.

Printed in the United States of America.
10 9 8 7 6 5 4 3 2 1

ISBN: 978-1-950743-25-4

Cover by Jon Van Amber
Book design by Gary Lindberg

Care Under Fire

Bill Strusinski

This book is dedicated to my brothers and sisters who have faithfully discharged their military duties as a combat medic by rendering "Care Under Fire." I also want to salute the men and women of the First Infantry Division, and the 26th Infantry Regiment, who for more than one hundred years have shed blood on battle fields throughout the world in defense of America and freedom. I honor every veteran who served for we all are true patriots.

It was my privilege to be a Blue Spader in the Big Red One in Vietnam. We cared for each other, we fought together, we grieved together. Some died, many were wounded and all of us were sentenced to a life of remembering all of it. As a medic, I was honored to be there to care for my brothers. Some of you I could help, some of you I could not, but all of us did our best to serve God and our Country.

The spirit of the "Fighting First" is articulated in its motto:

"No Mission Too Difficult.
No Sacrifice Too Great.
Duty First!"

The 26th Infantry Regiment, the Blue Spaders, are known for their Regimental spirit of

"Courage, Resourceful Daring, and Relentless Pursuit of the Enemy."

"Once a Blue Spader, always a Blue Spader."

Table of Contents

Preface

"I will admit I was afraid of going into battle, but at least I had my brothers."

This is my story. It is totally written from my perspective. I am not a journalist, a historian, or a general, although it would be fun to be one for a few days. I love America and the men and women who served in the First Infantry Division.

Calvin Coolidge once said, "A nation that forgets its defenders will itself be forgotten." Fortunately, through the adversity and trauma the Vietnam War has caused, veterans have not allowed our government to forget about us. We did our job and tried to serve as real peacemakers. In combat, we believed we were the best that we could ever be. Vietnam veterans also possessed the proverbial "Vietnam chip on our shoulders," which no doubt made us feel we were a cut above the rest.

My experiences during the war and the lessons I've learned have enabled me to appreciate and live a fuller life. I hope that my story will help readers understand my progression as a citizen and how my military experiences continue to strengthen the foundation of my professional life as a government executive, political strategist and lobbyist.

One of the goals of this book is to provide context about what it was like to be a combat medic. I tried to capture what I did, how I felt at the time, and some of the personal lessons I learned. Another goal is to highlight the special bond that existed between me as a medic and my brothers-in-arms. I've discussed this relationship with other combat medics, and we all felt the same strong, special bond between ourselves and the soldiers we fought with. We all felt that special debt of gratitude from those who unwillingly were assigned to our care.

My original intent was simpler—to share my story with my family so they could better understand the impact of the Vietnam War on me so they could better understand my psyche and how I approach life. I soon realized the tremendous therapeutic benefits of writing about my experiences. The writing exercise enabled me to deal with a few issues that have been bothering me since I left Vietnam in 1968. Putting my thoughts on paper helped me revisit some of my war memories of fear, anxiety, exhaustion and remorse, all of which contributed to my repertoire of life's lessons.

I have witnessed men's worst behavior and also many acts of compassion that showed civility in combat. To move beyond the horrors of war, I found myself tucking away the nastiness into small compartments in my mind. I call one of these compartments "my demon corner." These demons are always there, but they don't get out much anymore. Instead, I have chosen to focus more on the lessons that have added value to my life. I've allowed the positive lessons and valuable insights I gained in combat to meander freely in my mind unencumbered by pitfalls or roadblocks.

Even though I was trained as a medic, I was still part of an infantry unit and vividly remember the things we did and why and how we did them. I am not trying to pass myself off as a scholar on military tactics, but it doesn't take an academic military background to explain the most fundamental combat tasks we executed. I did occasionally research my remembrances so I could validate my recollections and complete my thoughts. All in all, writing my story was an enjoyable exercise and helped bring closure to some of the more complicated issues that have troubled me.

I sincerely want my reflections to serve as a tribute to all those millions of lives affected by the Vietnam War. Civil unrest in America was not just protests in the streets but discussions in every home and arguments in every workplace. I am forever hopeful the political demands made by a protesting public will prove sufficient to change society and our approach to military conflict.

My story is about family, patriotism and unconditional love of country. While in Vietnam, I may have disagreed with some of the political approaches to solving problems, but that goes with the territory. All soldiers are fully aware of the responsibility our government has to "protect and promote the common defense." That Bill of Rights proclamation runs deep in the minds and hearts of our defenders. Those who served were indeed ready to make the ultimate sacrifice. We didn't want to, nor did we ever think it would happen, but down deep, we all were ready to step into the hereafter if need be.

Chapter 1

A Year Condensed to Reflections

- I hate snakes!
- Why is it so hot?
- Does it ever stop raining?
- How many days left in country?
- Will I be brave?
- Will I make mom and dad proud?
- Are we really patriots?
- Lord, don't let me fall asleep on my watch.
- Lord, don't let me screw-up.
- Why do firefights seem like organized chaos with lots of noise?
- Did someone yell "medic?"
- Where's my morphine pack?
- Where the hell is that "dust-off?"
- Why are night ambush patrols full of terror and frequent mayhem?
- Remember to pull the pin before you throw.
- B-52 bombs sure make big holes in the ground.
- A sucking chest wound really does suck. Thank God for petroleum gauze battle bandages.
- When it came to sutures, the baseball stich was my favorite!
- Wow, my training didn't prepare me for this.

- Once a Blue Spader, always a Blue Spader!
- Duty First!

In sorting through my experiences during my tour of duty, I prepared the list of expressions above, all of which will be immediately recognized by those who served. Each reference communicates some aspect of my story in concise terms covering 366 days in a combat zone. These declarations run the gauntlet of my experience and summarize my feelings.

As they say, I survived my time in hell. I gathered wisdom and learned to understand what it means to be courageous. I felt the burdensome pain of worry and the full effects of heartache. I did and experienced things that most young adults can't begin to envision.

Perhaps they should not.

Chapter 2

Dear Family

I am a lucky guy. From my parents, I learned about the meaning of life and the importance and benefits of being virtuous and kind. I count my blessings every day. I have enormous gratitude for the rock-solid upbringing I received. My mother taught me compassion and provided unconditional love, even when the condition should have been questioned.

My mother, Jackie, was a motivator and problem solver. She didn't suffer fools and insisted that honesty and integrity be the order of the day. Her value system was well-established. She believed, "There is never a burden so great that you cannot handle it if you simply approach it with consideration and love." She made me understand, "A spoken word cannot be recalled, so in anger, be quiet."

Mom was the one who encouraged me to take risks and spread my wings. She used to tell me to "Go forth and do good things, learn from your mistakes and be nice to everyone you meet." She was a considerate soul who always took in stray dogs and kids. She was a smart, tenacious woman of high integrity who was an excellent role model for any person who had the good fortune to enter her circle of life.

My father, Will, taught me about the significance of completing a task regardless of how difficult or confusing it was. He taught me the value of sticking up for myself and others. He taught me to deal with adversity—that "life ain't fair!" He taught me about working hard, the value of working smart, and how to make a buck and reap the rewards of my labor. Like all dads, though, he questioned how I spent my frugal cash on trivial things.

There was something very wholesome about our upbringing back then. We were a family and part of a community of families who simply wanted to enjoy a better life and learn when to take advantage of new opportunities. To me, this was true. I still find much comfort in reflecting on my young, formative years. The support and encouragement I received from my parents and older brother gave me the confidence to take on the dangerous challenges life would send my way.

I consider myself fortunate to have learned right from wrong at an early age—even though the two concepts seemed to conflict at times. I even learned it was not nice to blame my older brother for my misdeeds. Falsehoods were met with metered punishment ranging from "getting grounded" to "getting whipped with the belt." I always hated that brand of personal education, so I eventually conformed my actions to the rules of the house. On the scale of punishment, I remember that brushing my teeth with soap ranked somewhere in the middle. Such methods to educate were easy to execute and highly effective. I suspect that all the children in our neighborhood were educated the same way. After all, it was the 1950s, and it truly was a village raising the local kids. As young men, my brother and I were well-educated on taking responsibility for our own actions.

Although I've not always succeeded, I have consistently tried to keep everyday problems in perspective. The crisis-solving skills I developed in Vietnam taught me to take my time and assess the risks and the rewards before acting or making major decisions. I have learned not to sweat the small stuff. I still make my bed immediately upon rising every morning so I can begin each day by completing the first task.

I try not to argue but to observe. I try to educate and exchange ideas in a manner that adheres to the ethics of respect and decency. I strive to remain calm in a crisis but nevertheless always look for the nearest exit.

On the downside, I have learned to keep my emotions in check. Although I have passion to support my beliefs, my emotional aptitude is probably less than it should be. I have feelings, but a lot of times I don't show them or talk about them. I have been known to disengage and not communicate with someone I have a conflict with. These are the lessons I learned as a medic in a combat infantry company.

During my year in Vietnam, I learned the importance of personal discipline and bravery. I learned how to cope with the fear of combat and understand the need to be grateful for surviving. I witnessed many extraordinary, selfless acts of bravery and remarkable courage. Maybe, on occasion, I was courageous myself, but certainly not on purpose. When you are under fire, your training and previous experiences enable you to take the required action. When the gunfire subsides, you engage your brain and think about your next steps to either care for the injured or help you and your casualty survive the situation. Sometimes, it worked out, and other times it did not.

As medics, we were focused on doing our jobs. At times, it was a heavy burden due to the life or death nature of the work. Out of necessity, medics unselfishly respond to the anguished call for "MEDIC!" and cautiously advance to the scene of the carnage to witness the injury and surrounding chaos. That's when adrenaline kicks in, and medics take charge by rendering aid to the best of their abilities.

Sometimes, as a medic, it is necessary to fire your weapon to defend yourself or protect your patient. Survival is a powerful motivator. Getting your battle-injured companion to safety and medical treatment provides a powerful incentive to do what needs to be done. Upon occasion, I fought the enemy, which is the goal of combat. Now, when I look back on those events, it seems that trying to kill someone who was trying to kill me was too automatic—but highly necessary. Over the years, I've thought about my attempts to take another man's life who was just following orders to take mine. I believe that I did the right thing, but those actions were accompanied by lifelong and weighty reflections.

Chapter 3

And Now It Begins—Drafted

I must point out, "We were soldiers once and young," and the past is very much alive within us. Issues surrounding the Vietnam War, both at home and abroad, affected the very fabric of our democracy, challenged many of our governmental institutions and dramatically impacted veterans and citizens alike. It tested our resolve and brought into question our right to pursue the happiness guaranteed in the Bill of Rights. For many of us, reconciliation has been a lifelong process.

Putting battle scars into perspective remains a challenge, no matter how long we have been separated from the battlefield. I think of my brothers-in-arms and the unique experiences we shared. Most veterans learn to deal with those traumatic experiences and lead somewhat normal lives. Others have not been so fortunate and find it very difficult to be productive citizens. The memories and heartache of those days in a war zone is constant for all of us, and it is concealed just below the surface of our reflections.

I graduated from Hill High School in St. Paul, which was a fine parochial school for boys. I received a quality education and learned how to solve problems and deal with challenges. I learned the importance of becoming disciplined to achieve results. And I developed some study skills. *Go Pioneers!* After high school, I enrolled at Mankato State College about a hundred miles south of St.

Paul. I was the first in my family to go to college, and I looked forward to expanding both my mindset and my skillset so I could make good money when I graduated.

During my early college days, I worked on my general education requirements and tried to decide on a major. While my grades were passing, some influences outside of academics started to divert my focus away from studying. Having graduated from an all-male high school, I began exploring these adolescent urges and trying to understand the female mindset. I am still trying to complete that analysis. After all, the pursuit of a higher education obligates a person to undertake the unquestionable search for happiness and the true "meaning of life!" Remember, this was the 60's, and free love and peace were the mantras of our existence.

In October 1966, I had to withdraw from college due to an illness that put me in the hospital. It was my sophomore year, and I was just getting in the groove of my late teen years. Since I failed to meet the minimum requirements for maintaining my student deferment, I became eligible for the draft. I received my 1A, "eligible for the draft" change-in-status notice in November, and in December 1966, I received a very official-looking letter from the federal government.

As was the custom, the letter started out as follows, "Greetings from the President of the United States......" *Wow, I've just been drafted!* Women, fun, fast cars, the library, smart professors with words of wisdom, and campus parties were officially over. My youthful quest for happiness, truth and justice was about to enter a new dimension.

When I received my draft notice, I really didn't think much about it because my dad and several uncles served in the military during WWII. My uncle Tut was a night fighter radar specialist who fought the Japanese as his Marine Fighter Squadron island-hopped in the Pacific Theater. Serving in the military and serving your country is just what we did. We were expected to answer the call to duty, and we did.

My older brother was called into service but was injured in a car accident the week before he was to leave for basic training. His broken shoulder changed his eligibility status to "physically unable to perform." That accident was deeply troubling to him. He was looking forward to going into the Army. He talked about this frustration and missing his chance to serve our country and prove-up his manhood. He would have made a good soldier. I am speaking about this because he was very supportive of my service and proud of my accomplishments. Mike was a great older brother who died at 61. His encouragement and thoughtfulness were deeply appreciated by me, the younger brother, as it should be.

As a footnote and a sign of true family patriotism, both of my brother's sons, Tom and Gary, proudly served in the all-volunteer Army and faced combat in two different wars. My son, Bill, wanted to join the Marines but suffered from a serious hip issue that disqualified him from military service. Too bad, he would have made a great Marine.

The bottom line—our family has a tradition of being willing to answer the call of duty. Maybe answering the call is just what descendants of Northern European immigrants do. After all, our grandparents had a very deep appreciation of the opportunities that living in America afforded them, and they all were willing to fight against tyranny.

Soon after I received my official draft notice, olive drab would become my new favorite color. I was excited to begin my adventure with the belief that the entire experience would surely be valuable and useful for the rest of my life. Little did I know at the time just how valuable these lessons would become. Even though I answered the call, upon reflection, I remember being both excited and apprehensive. I think all teenagers acknowledge this dilemma and worry about their ability to complete this "boy to man" transitional task. I wondered if I would be able to "man-up" and achieve the expected "warrior status."

I was particularly apprehensive about the physical stuff. You see, I did not possess, nor did I display any athletic prowess during my four years in high school. I was overweight and generally lacked the kind of discipline I expected the Army would require. In the end, my apprehension and outright fear abated. My new-found self-confidence, combined with the love and support of my family and friends, propelled me to new heights of patriotism. Such thinking was new to me. Armed with these new understandings, I was ready to continue along my journey through life. Thus, I was excited for my new military adventure to begin. Little did I know it would be quite a chapter in my life's voyage.

Chapter 4

The Induction Ceremony

On March 13, 1967, I was sworn in at the Armory in St. Paul, located in the Minnesota State Capitol complex. I took the sacred oath "to faithfully discharge my duties and to uphold and support the Constitution of the United States." I never gave much thought to the allegiance I was pledging—it was just something I did. Hell, we all did it. After all, we were teenagers, we were untested, and we were believers. Besides, most of us were drafted and couldn't imagine moving to Canada to avoid our responsibilities as a child of Uncle Sam. Years later, my unquestioning willingness to follow orders by my military and government leaders gave way to a reexamination of major government policies and the justifications supporting them.

My dad, a WWII veteran, drove me to the Armory to be sworn in, which ultimately led to me being sworn at a lot. Dad was a quiet man about all things personal. His job in a local steel foundry was hard and hot, no matter the time of year. He was one of nine children born to Polish immigrants. He grew into a proud man who earned enough money for our family to live comfortably in a house he built on the East Side of St. Paul. I remember him being firm when he needed to be but just as often willing to give the shirt off his back to strangers. He never showed much emotion, and he certainly wasn't the kind of dad who gave us "as you go through life" speeches.

With this in mind, imagine my surprise on the way to the induction when Dad said he wanted to share some advice on how the Army works, how to deal with the challenges that lie ahead, and especially how to survive the entire ordeal. I was suddenly filled with excitement and anticipation. This was going to be our first real man-to-man talk. Dad was about to give me advice that would be profound and serve me a lifetime. I just knew it would be good advice because he survived the Army and received an honorable discharge from Uncle Sam in 1946.

As Dad parked the car in front of the Armory, he grabbed my shoulder to emphasize the importance of what he was about to say. "Listen up, Son. This is how you can survive the Army. Keep your mouth shut and do what you're told!"

I sat silently and reflected on his heartfelt advice. Honestly, my first thought was, *Really? That's it? Where's the AHA moment I was expecting? Where is the "as you go through life, take it to the bank" advice?* I was a bit disappointed because this was the same instruction my dad had been giving me since I was five years old! While it was not the counsel I was anticipating, it was, in the final analysis, excellent advice. I faithfully followed Dad's pearl of wisdom, and sure enough, I was able to do my duty, fulfill my Army obligation and secure an Honorable Discharge. To properly fulfill my obligation as a mentor to future generations, I have imparted this most excellent advice to my children and grandchildren. And I'm sure they were disappointed at first too.

The Army doctors quickly gave me a physical exam and certified me as fit for service. Shortly thereafter, we stood in formation and took the oath. Standing in line, I felt some anxiety about what might lie ahead. My unease increased when every eighth inductee was directed to step out of line with no reason given. Once this new group was assembled, a sergeant announced in a sinister voice, "Welcome to the Marine Corps!" I did not know the military could just assign inductees to the marines, but they did. I was grateful not to be in that group. In hindsight, this probably was my first "close call." *Hooyah!*

Without a parade or even a band heralding our departure, we were loaded onto a bus and transported to the airport where we boarded a plane for Fort Campbell, Kentucky. I had never been to Kentucky before and it was March, so I figured the weather had to be better than it was in Minnesota. *Meeting new friends, traveling to Kentucky, three squares a day, serving my country—how fun.*

"I have never been so scared in my young life!"

Chapter 5

Basic Training

Basic training means a lot of hollering, vast quantities of push-ups, countless chin-ups, mud, wet, cold, miles of running and learning the fundamental fighting skills needed to be a member of the infantry. The shooting part was nifty, but the exercise part was a big challenge. The initial physical training test (PT) clearly demonstrated that I had a significant opportunity for improvement. I could do two push-ups and five sit-ups but no chin-ups. I couldn't run a block, let alone a mile.

I didn't want to be the one guy in the family to fail—how's that for motivation? I was already worried about failure. When it came right down to it, I wanted to prove my qualifications and make my family proud. Besides, the Army hopes to create leaders out of each solider, so they won't let you fail. In basic training, you quickly develop a "can do" attitude that motivates you to do the seemingly unimaginable. I knew that graduating from basic training was my only option, so I decided this was my chance to finally get into physical shape for the first time.

It was an adventure, alright. The hollering, push-ups and low crawling through mud continued day and night. We ran everywhere and spent huge amounts of time running the obstacle course and chasing each other through the hills and swamps of Kentucky. Surprisingly, we never ran into any moonshiners.

It turns out that lots of pain actually meant lots of gain. I couldn't believe my physical transformation and the mental toughness I was gaining, a quality that would prove critical in combat. I developed confidence in my newfound abilities, which made my personal self-esteem soar.

I came to be proud that my training took place at Fort Campbell, which is the home of the 101st Airborne Division. The drill instructors were Airborne elite. They knew their job and trained us well. Looking back, I guess they knew we were headed to combat in Vietnam, so they wanted to prepare us to survive.

Ironically, several months after basic training, my company greeted a battalion of "Screaming Eagles" of the 101st Airborne Division when they initially arrived in Vietnam. My unit was securing the base camp at Phouc Vinh. While walking down the perimeter roadway, I ran into my basic training platoon sergeant. We exchanged pleasantries and "small world" greetings, but he had twenty years under his Army belt at that time and was not happy to have been levied to Vietnam.

In basic training, I started as part of a group of unorganized, apprehensive boys from all around the country. We represented every conceivable walk of life and shared the common bond of fearing our futures. In just eight weeks, the dedicated drill instructors molded us into "men" and a military fighting unit. By week eight, we could march in perfect unison, exercise all day and shoot straight. To a man, we felt competent in our abilities and well-adjusted to all things Army.

During basic training, we were given a battery of tests that somehow determined the military occupational job specialties (MOS) we would be assigned to. Further training in an MOS determined one's Army job and next duty assignment. After my test results were analyzed, I was interviewed by an Army education specialist and initially offered several training choices ranging from cannon cocker (artillery) to infantry.

There were two types of people who served in the Army at that time. Trust me, each group was treated differently. The Regular Army (RA) soldiers were those who voluntarily enlisted for three years while the draftees (US) were only required to serve two years active duty. The better jobs seemed to favor the RA guys. As a draftee, my choices were somewhat limited. I was offered jobs as truck driver, infantry, artillery, mechanized infantry, cook, clerk, radio operator, and general maintenance worker, to name a few. My couple of years in college didn't seem to make any difference to those in charge.

My job choices didn't seem very appealing. *What to do?* "Hey sarge, mind if I call home and talk this over with my mom? She's a smart lady and could give me excellent advice."

Sarge's response to such naïve requests was always along the line of: "NO, MORON! Drop and give me fifty push-ups!" *Why did they always want fifty push-ups and not five?*

To understand my ultimate job decision, I need to provide a little context. This was the 1960s, and my generation was exposed to a lot of TV that only seemed to broadcast Westerns and war flicks and a few military mini-series. In my youth, WWII was still fresh in the public's mind. The public believed WWII was a just and noble war. The personal stories of combat soldiers were the subjects of good television in the 50s and early 60s. TV was the perfect medium to highlight the courage and heroism of soldiers and civilian leaders alike. These reflections made all of us feel proud to be Americans.

"Combat Medic" was the name of a popular weekly TV series that featured medics in combat. The medics were the stars and always in the middle of the action. They were the heroes who saved lives and comforted the wounded. Soldiers admired and protected the medics. The show was very popular, and I know my love for it influenced my choice of MOS. I volunteered to be a medic.

The education specialist and sergeant promptly agreed to my request. Since they showed no hesitation, I have always wondered if they received a bonus or a coveted three-day pass for my decision.

Anyway, I already knew how to drive, shoot and shovel, so working in a hospital seemed like a way to learn useful skills at government expense.

I also concluded that learning emergency first aid would be a valuable skill to have. Of course, the sergeant's tip that I could put in for hospital duty in Italy or Germany may have influenced me too. *Now I am getting somewhere,* I thought. *This Army life won't be so bad after all.*

Unfortunately, I soon discovered that when a draftee put in for a duty assignment, it was seen as merely a suggestion. It certainly didn't obligate the higher-ups to honor my request. Uncle Sam was free to send me anywhere he desired, and that sorry Uncle eventually did just that.

After I said yes to medical training, I was told I'd become certified as a combat medic (91B). With that decision out of the way, my military adventure was about to begin in earnest.

In week seven of basic training, our skills and personal resolve were tested to the max during the Army's version of "Hell Week." By now, I had ample reason to consider every week in the Army as "Hell Week." *What else could the hardcore Airborne drill instructors possibly conjure up to make our miserable lives even more miserable?* In retrospect, "Hell Week" was a great name for this required training exercise because it aptly described all activities nasty and difficult.

We marched through the forests and swamps of Kentucky, scratching our itches and rubbing our sore feet. With a buddy, we set up pup tents each night and went to sleep worrying about spiders and watching out for snakes. I saw a couple of water moccasins or cottonmouths on the first day of our excursion, which guaranteed I wouldn't sleep the entire time we were on bivouac. But we survived, and nobody got bitten or severely injured. The harsh commands of the drill sergeants gave way to more supportive encouragement. I remember feeling boundless pride after completing that exercise. I suspect the drill sergeants were just relieved that none of us died.

By the end of basic training, our ragtag cast of characters had all survived knowing we were better for it. We had passed the book-learning part and overcome the obstacle course. I could do fifty push-ups, fifty chin-ups, run a mile in under seven minutes and had earned an Expert Marksman Badge with the M-14 rifle. *What a transition!* Best of all, I was proud to be in the Army, proud to wear my uniform and ready to serve my country.

Graduation day was truly special. We were an impressive bunch and looked good right down to our spit-shined boots. We were survivors. We had not failed. We had earned the right to be called soldiers.

It was a beautiful day full of sunshine, excitement and generals. We marched in perfect cadence around the parade field and expertly saluted the flag and Army brass. As the band played "The Stars and Stripes Forever," we all beamed with the kind of pride that can best be appreciated by those who had completed basic training before us.

Hooray, we made it! I lost sixty-five pounds during those eight weeks. I felt positive and accomplished. I remember thinking, *Basic training really wasn't that bad. Hell, man, after that experience I can do anything!*

The next part of my adventure was moving on to advanced individual training (AIT) and a new training post. Because an eventual hospital assignment in Europe was still a possibility, I couldn't wait for my training as a medic to start.

Chapter 6

Advanced Individual Training

I was given two weeks' leave between basic training and AIT. But hanging out with my civilian buddies soon led to boredom. I was excited to learn new skills and continue my Army adventure. Leave ended soon enough, and I traveled by commercial air to my new duty station in San Antonio. Fort Sam Houston, affectionately called Ft. Sam, is named for Sam Houston, a well-known hero and military strategist who died at the Alamo, which is also located in San Antonio.

Ft. Sam is the major training facility for all medical staff in the US Army. The hospital at Ft. Sam is still described as one of the best health care facilities in the country for soldiers and veterans. It also has a solid reputation as one of the elite burn treatment hospitals in the country. Their extensive treatment of catastrophic combat burn injuries put them on the cutting edge of research and the development of advanced protocols in the US.

Since I had never been to Texas, I had no idea what the weather would be like. I discovered that Texas is very hot in the summertime! When I got to my training unit, orientation included discussion on what to expect from the training cadre and the environment. I wasn't too concerned about the Army's agenda, but I didn't like having to add "watch out for rattlesnakes and scorpions" to my list of other worries. I ultimately concluded I would be trained in snakebite identification and treatment, so I relaxed a bit.

At the time I didn't know how practical my training on such eventualities would be—in Vietnam I did indeed treat soldiers for reptile encounters. The challenge in Texas was prophetic because every snake I encountered in Vietnam, and there were many, was poisonous—mostly pit vipers, which inject venom that attacks the blood system. Neuro-toxic venom bites, on the other hand, attack the nervous system and are very deadly and almost impossible to survive. Pit viper bites were nasty to handle, but I can report that everyone survived except for the snake.

My medical training lasted for ten weeks. I learned emergency first aid procedures and how to identify some basic maladies like pink eye and intestinal disruptions. I learned how to give shots and how to draw blood and start IVs. My training taught me how to use splints and tourniquets, how to treat for shock and apply battle dressings, how to take someone's temperature (orally and rectally) and how to measure a respiration rate and blood pressure. I learned how to use a stethoscope, how the heart and lungs sound in a well person, how to suture and do a modified tracheotomy. And, of course, I learned about bedpans and how to fill out a shot record and battle injury tag.

The whole time I was in the Army, other than a couple of days of learning hospital procedures, I never stepped inside a hospital. Like my training, most of my medical experiences in the Army were rendering emergency care in the field.

There was an intense physical component to supplement our classroom training. We were evaluated on such things as the "fireman's carry" and the "stretcher exercise." Not only did we jog for miles at a time, but we learned the proper technique to safely transport a wounded soldier on a stretcher or on our back. We became experts at carrying a 180-pound casualty over rough terrain, up and down endless stairs and out of ditches. We climbed rope ladders and scaled obstacles. We were pushed to the limits in 110-degree heat and without much sleep. I must admit, the training proved invaluable and prepared me for the real-life experiences that were in my combat future.

In the final analysis, my time at Fort Sam was well spent but only exposed me to a minimum set of practices, protocols and techniques. During my ten-week AIT, I was only taught the fundamentals of emergency aide. Like most military occupations, the Army recognized that "on-the-job" training would enhance my medical capabilities. After all, how in the hell can you train someone in Texas on what it's like to treat a casualty under combat circumstances? You can't. I have been through training, and I have been through combat. Learning how to deal with the emotional stress and chaotic aspects of combat is a self-developed skill that can only come from "on-the-job training."

Combat was both mental and physical. You gain experience, and you develop confidence. I was amazed to discover how much aide I could render with what, at times, seemed like so little training.

AIT graduation day was also very special and proved again that I could complete a challenge and build self-esteem. The feeling of accomplishment was immense. Most importantly, Graduation Day was when I would finally get my Army duty assignment. I was especially excited to be moving out of the "low life trainee" phase of my military career and into a real job.

I was dripping with sweat on the parade field at Fort Sam on a hot July day. Our chests were puffed out, and our heads held high. We were part of a new elite group and very proud. Once the ceremony concluded, it was time to get our next assignment. I remember thinking, *Wow, this is it. This is what I have been training and waiting for the past six months.* I was not apprehensive, because I remained focused on hospital duty in Italy! My thoughts were on learning to speak Italian and enjoying fine Italian cuisine.

Finally, as we stood at attention and cooked in the hot Texas sun, our assignments were distributed. The battalion commander congratulated each of us as he presented our Medic Certificates, acknowledging our competency as combat medics. *Cool.* But I am thinking, *Where are the duty station assignment orders?* According to the Army, we were deemed "capable of doing the job." *Thanks for the kudos and the Graduation Certificate, but where are my duty station orders?*

It was difficult to control my enthusiasm—with my pounding heart, it might be better to say to control my anxiety. Without any more fanfare or further reflection, I was given my orders. *But what do they mean?* They seemed to be written in code. I didn't understand them, so I reluctantly approached my first sergeant and asked, "What is Headquarters Company, 1st Battalion, 26th Infantry, 1st Infantry Division?"

First sergeant said, "Son, you've been assigned to an infantry unit in Vietnam. You're hereby declared to be a combat medic."

Holy shit, is this really happening? Yup! So, I asked, "What about my request for a hospital assignment in Germany or Italy?"

"Son, the Army is always open to requests but never duty bound by such trivia," first sergeant replied loudly enough so others could hear. "The Army is very smart and knows best how to deploy its personnel resources."

I had one more question but, at this point, felt it might fall on deaf ears. I showed the first sergeant a copy of my personal files. On the front cover jacket, stamped in big, red letters, was the statement: "NOT QUALIFIED FOR COMBAT DUTY." *Surely that would favor my reassignment to hospital duty somewhere.*

The first sergeant took my file and studied the contents, uncovering the reason for that "unqualified" notation. With a look of pride only a first sergeant can exhibit, he said, "Look here. It says you have bad eyesight and need to wear glasses. That's the reason. But hold on, I can fix that!" He directed his company clerk to order me three additional pairs of glasses and make sure one pair was sunglasses. He ended our little Q&A and abruptly dismissed me.

I thought, *Now would be a good time to bend over and kiss my sorry ass goodbye.*

But being a positive person, I told myself to just "suck it up—after all, it's only a year in Vietnam." My positivity, however, took a small hit when I realized that my one-year tour was during leap year, meaning I'd be in Vietnam 366 days instead of the typical 365 days.

My dream of working at a hospital in Italy was not to be. I surrendered to the will of Uncle Sam. Actually, I had no choice—my life now belonged to Uncle Sam. In front of the first sergeant, I did my best to demonstrate that my enthusiasm for the Army's intelligent assignment matched my new obligation. I'm sure I failed.

Chapter 7

Welcome to Vietnam and the Big Red One

The flight over to Vietnam was but another new experience. We crossed the international date line and peered endlessly into the ocean, hoping to spot land, ships or large creatures. We refueled in Hawaii and Okinawa but didn't have any time to explore or relax. I have never been on a flight that lasted twenty-four hours. Our stewardesses treated us with the utmost respect and kindness. They were professionals who enjoyed their job. They appeared happy, but looking back, that was most likely their way of dealing with the stress of giving a ride to young boys about to enter battle. Some displayed tendencies like those of our mothers, which was comforting. I suspect they knew more about what we were getting into than we did. Other "stews" seemed like the girl we all wanted to be waiting for us when we returned home.

We were given plenty of food. The very long flight also gave us plenty of time to think about what we were going to miss about our civilian life. Down deep, we all knew our lives would be forever changed, so we began to focus upon the challenges that lie ahead. No matter what, the plane was not turning around, and our own individual destiny would soon be realized. It was a crazy time because none of us knew what the hell to expect. After serving in the Army for six months, I knew that uncertainty was certainty and the enormity of my challenges was definitely increasing.

Eventually, our transport touched down at Tan Son Nhut Air Base in Saigon. *Goodbye world and hello Vietnam!* When the doors opened and we exited the plane, I was instantly accosted by colossal heat and the accompanying smells of high humidity and war. I immediately began longing for the comforts of home and loving arms of family. It finally occurred to me that it was going to be a very long year of service to my country.

A few mortars were aimlessly launched by the enemy and landed some distance away from our plane. But that common incident was clearly a signal for us to de-board the craft as quickly as possible. We offloaded to waiting buses that had chicken wire covering the windows. I thought that that was curious, so I asked our driver the reason for the decoration. He responded, "You are obviously a new guy in country, and Uncle Sam needs you to take the place of some other GI who is going home. The chicken wire, dumb ass, is to prevent grenades thrown at the bus by VC assassins from landing inside and killing you before you even get to take your first crap in Vietnam." *Oh, lucky me.* I now knew the answer to what I thought was a logical inquiry. Suffice it to say, my humble curiosity was addressed by a soldier driver who had been asked that question a million times before. We eventually made it to Division Headquarters at Dian where my orientation and transportation up-country to my unit would be arranged.

Soon enough, I arrived at the Division Headquarters of the 1st Infantry Division, aka the Big Red One (BRO). This highly decorated division is well known throughout history and is the oldest continuously serving combat unit in the Army dating back to its first commander, General Pershing. Formed during the Spanish-American War, the "Fighting First" led the way in WWI and WWII. During WWI, this division fought at Cantigny, and this decisive battle finally turned the tide of the war in favor of the allies.

In WWII, this proud and highly decorated division fought the Germans in Africa, Sicily and Italy and led the D-Day invasion into France via Normandy and Omaha Beach. They fought their way to the Ardennes Forest and contributed to the major success of German defeat during the Battle of the Bulge.

The BRO Division spent five years in Vietnam. It was the first full division to deploy to Vietnam in September 1965. The division rotated back to Fort Riley, Kansas, in 1970. The "Fighting First," due to the resolve of its combatants and the quality of its leaders, made significant battle contributions in WWII and Vietnam. All soldiers were well trained and committed to serving country and safeguarding their brothers in arms. As soldiers, our goals were simple. We wanted to do our job to the best of our ability and to get safely back home to the "good life."

For those who believed the myth that fighting in Vietnam was much less intense than WWII, please understand this one fact. Sadly enough, the First Infantry Division suffered more battle causalities in Vietnam than they did in WWII. War is hell, no matter where it is fought! Regrettably, the public had concluded WWII was a noble and just war, and Vietnam was not. Try telling that to the soldiers who served in the Big Red One. The two wars were vastly different in their approaches to combat. For example, in WWII, combat took place on a sizable geographical front that involved many soldiers and units.

During WWII, the BRO was deployed in North Africa, Sicily and Italy. The division eventually made its way to Germany via Normandy on D-Day. These were larger battles that were fought along a clearly defined battlefront. The approach was to take and occupy and defend as much land possible. In Vietnam, there was no defined front that separated us from the enemy. Our goal was not to occupy battle won terrain but to kill as many enemy as possible and then withdraw. Guerilla warfare required a new kind of battle tactic that took time to evolve. Our battles involved smaller fighting units but occurred with much more frequency. In both wars, the soldiers of the Big Red One made sacrifices and earned their deserved place in American military history. In WWII, the soldiers of the BRO were brave and paved the way for us while doing their jobs to defend our country and promote freedom. They helped eliminate a tyrant who had no morals and was motivated by the lust of ruling the world.

Even though they were two different wars with two different outcomes, I did not realize an important fact until I did a little research. It didn't take long to discover the average soldiers of the BRO in WWII experienced combat forty times in four years. In Vietnam, the average infantryman was in combat 240 times in one year. This statistic explains why there were so many more overall casualties taken by the BRO in Vietnam than in WWII. Soldiers of the 1st have always made tremendous sacrifices to preserve freedom. I am making this comparison for those people who thought the Vietnam War was merely a conflict, limited in scope and "no big deal!" The Vietnam War was truly much more than a conflict. The battle causalities were enormous, the sacrifices were immense and the lasting impact on the participants immeasurable. Vietnam was not "just" a conflict, as many politicians described it. Vietnam was a war plain and simple. No matter what superficial description that has been applied to our involvement in Vietnam, we, as soldiers, did our job. Regardless of the war, in combat, you learn about the fragility of life and the complexities of surviving with your spirit intact. Perhaps that explains why so many veterans live life to the fullest and express feelings in a more intense manner.

The Big Red One Division was positioned north and west of Saigon all the way to the Cambodian border. My base camp, Quan Loi, was only four miles from Cambodia. Our mission was to engage and destroy the enemy coming down the Ho Chi Minh Trail and disrupt their ability to enter Saigon. Our job was to interrupt their supply chain and troop replacements. It was a low, mountainous geographical area consisting of heavy jungle and a relatively sparse civilian population. Our area of operation was mostly agricultural with mostly small villages and hamlets. This area provided excellent terrain in which to conceal enemy troop movements. The conditions were ideal for the enemy to construct undetectable underground base camps and trails to move troops and supplies almost at will. There was always a division of the North Vietnamese Army (NVA) determined to fight us in this free-wheeling battle sector.

In Vietnam, the 1st Infantry Division repeatedly proved itself in combat. This great and gallant division consistently fought with pride and integrity. Like every battle ever fought by the Big Red One in previous wars in the past, we never lost a battle, we never lost sight of our mission and we never forgot our brothers. We took care of each other. Sure, we felt patriotic and loyal to our country, but we felt more loyal to each other. We learned from those that served before us. Our combat predecessors set a high standard. Whether it was on the beaches of France or the jungles of Vietnam, the Big Red One continuously proved its worth and furthered its rock-solid combat reputation.

From August 1967 to 1968, it was my turn in the barrel. I will admit to apprehension when I stepped off the airplane in Saigon and smelled the heat, humidity and cordite. I was transported to division headquarters in Dian, where I was immediately sent to a five-day "jungle survival school." Little did I know jungle school would prove to be a precursor as to what lies ahead. Remember, the first principal of Army training was to learn practical skills while getting the hell scared out of you at the same time!

After jungle school, I was sent to Phouc Vinh about ninety miles northeast of Saigon, where I finally joined my battalion of Blue Spaders. A couple of months later, my battalion was ordered to move to Quan Loi to clear and secure an area for a new base camp built for us. The good news was we had a brand-new base camp, but the bad news was we were now smack dab in the middle of the key enemy route to Saigon. This meant we went from simple living conditions with barracks and buildings as our living quarters to even more humble conditions where we lived in tents surrounded by sandbags, which were literally on the perimeter of the camp. Although I remember spending most of our time living in fox holes in some godforsaken Night Defensive Position in the field, at least it was easy to get into the defensive position whenever the need arose. We did have sandbags around the tents we slept in, but all of us felt more comfortable in the bunkers, which were very close to our front and rear screen doors.

Quan Loi is near the Cambodian border, and we were missioned to stop the North Vietnamese Army infiltration across the border into Vietnam. This area is also known as the "fishhook." On a map of South Vietnam, the border is shaped like a "fishhook." By 1970, this integral part of the Ho Chi Minh Trail became perhaps the top major supply depot for the North Vietnamese Army. This geographical description gained notoriety when the Vietnamese and US Army were ordered by President Nixon to invade Cambodia in 1970. The invasion force entered Cambodia through the "fishhook." Because of the number of NVA troops operating in the area and the importance of their supply depots to the war effort in and around Saigon, the "fishhook" area of operations was the site of many frequent and fierce battles.

In 1967 and 1968, this was to be the land of enemy engagement for my unit of the BRO. Over time, my unit set up many ambush sites along that trail. I can truthfully say, we did have success in our nighttime missions, but these types of patrols created the most difficult conditions for me to deal with casualties. Sometimes we had to survive the firefight in place and wait for the rest of the company to come to our position in the morning. I sure was happy to see all of my brothers' smiling faces.

Chapter 8

Entering the Fray

A Combat soldiers' prayer:

Yeah, though I walk through the Valley of the shadow of Death,
I will fear no evil for I am the evilest son-of-a-bitch in the Valley.

In mid-August 1967, I arrived at Headquarters Company, 1ˢᵗ Battalion/26ᵗʰ Regiment. I was not only a proud member of the Big Red One, I was also a part of the famous Blue Spader Regiment. With their Big Red One units, the Blue Spaders served longer in Vietnam than any other division. After five continuous years of combat, when the Blue Spaders received orders to return home in 1970, the regiment had earned eleven battle streamers, a Valorous Unit award and two Foreign Service awards, which could forever be displayed on its colors.

My new commanding officer ordered me to memorize the 1ˢᵗ Infantry Division Motto: "No mission too difficult. No sacrifice too great. Duty first!"

I couldn't help but wonder if that was a predictor of things to come. *Oh well, no turning back now.*

I was genuinely proud to join the Big Red One and the Blue Spader Regiment. This regiment has a deep and rich military history. Prior to

Vietnam, it had received many distinguished battle citations, fighting in more than thirty-five major campaigns since 1900. Understanding unit history was important in the military in which unit cohesiveness depended on past successes. The knowledge gained in combat was due to the previous sacrifices and lessons learned from so many that had gone before.

We wore our Big Red One patches on our uniforms. Our ranks and last names were stenciled in black to make it more difficult for the enemy to identify sergeants and officers, who were prime targets along with radio operators and medics. The Viet Cong (VC) and NVA believed killing officers, non-commissioned officers (sergeants), RTOs and medics would create chaos in the American force, thereby destroying its ability to fight back. Of course, the enemy had it wrong—all US soldiers are cross-trained and capable of maintaining unit discipline in a firefight. For example, if a platoon leader (a 2nd lieutenant) went down, the platoon sergeant would step up and take his place, continuing to lead us in battle. Brave men and capable leaders existed throughout the unit. I guess that is what makes American soldiers the best in the world. Although our leaders wanted to become somewhat invisible and blend in with the regular troops, I'm not sure it really made any difference.

Shortly after my arrival, enemy rockets hit the main ammo dump (storage area) where most of the base ammunition ordnance was stored. As ammo exploded, the concussions literally threw me to the ground. The smell of cordite filled the air and debris cascaded down, covering everything in a thick coat of red clay. A tall plume of fire and smoke rapidly filled the sky. It was a million-dollar fireworks display, and I had a front seat! Unfortunately, it would not be my last show. The ordnance continued to explode for more than an hour, and I'm sure the VC were proud of their accomplishment.

The destruction of that ammo dump was the most terrifying incident I had ever witnessed. No training could have prepared me for such an experience. Fortunately, no one was injured. Hard to believe,

I know, but that was the case during many hostile activities. *Welcome to the Big Red One!*

A few days later, Company B (Bravo Company) tracked down the enemy unit that had attacked our ammo dump. The firefight lasted a couple of hours. Bravo Company put a real crimp in the enemy's style, hampering the VC's ability to carry out such attacks in the future. This should have meant a couple of months, at least.

After suffering major losses, the enemy usually retreated to Cambodia to rest, resupply and secure replacement troops. We thought the actions of Bravo Company had eliminated them as an immediate threat to our base camp, but that would soon change. New NVA recruits were already moving down the Ho Chi Minh Trail into our sector of operations. At the time, we didn't know the NVA was staging for a major operation during the Vietnamese New Year, more commonly known as TET.

At base camp, as soon as the fires burned out and the ammo dump was deemed safe, the ammo depot area was rebuilt. Soldiers are smart and resourceful—they learn from mistakes. Fortunately, they applied the "deficiency lessons" to make the new ammo depot better and stronger. In the Army, adversity and destruction provide excellent tutorials for improving the next facility to be built.

Simultaneously with the rebuilding project, new ordnance was flown in and conditions returned to normal, which meant that 155mm and 175mm howitzers once again began spitting reconnaissance fire to disrupt enemy supply trails. This made it virtually impossible to sleep while in basecamp.

After a few days of working at the battalion aide station, I was assigned by the battalion surgeon to Company A, where I would spend the next ten months as a field medic. I moved my few possessions to the company area and met the men of Lima Platoon, where I would serve until I became the Company A senior aidman.

The men of Lima Platoon were seasoned professionals and looked at me with skepticism because I was a newbie. They knew I'd never been in combat and had a right to question if I was capable of treating them when injured by enemy fire. I had the same concerns. In a combat unit, an unwritten rule requires the new guy to prove himself capable of performing under fire.

Soon, our unit got into a skirmish with me as the field medic. I did not run away, and I took care of business. This elite fighting unit quickly accepted me, and I earned the title of combat veteran— maybe because I had simply survived the ordeal. During the skirmish, I learned that staying calm was the only way to effectively treat a wounded brother and protect myself no matter how serious the injury or how much combat chaos was occurring around me.

One of the major tasks of an infantry soldier was to participate in nighttime ambush patrols. Stealth and speed were essential for the success of such patrols, so we frequently lightened our loads and adjusted our mindset to night conditions. I received a beret to wear on night operations instead of my helmet. I felt extremely proud when I first put on the green camouflage beret with the Blue Spader name embossed in gold thread. I wore that beret on many nighttime ambush patrols. Although it did not provide much protection, it reduced the noise of my steel pot rattling through the bush. The beret was also much cooler than my helmet. Although it was a misnomer, we all thought our berets also made us look "cool" and more menacing to the enemy. Comfort over protection was a common trait among infantry soldiers. No one ever accused us of applying good management principals to our ground-pounding routine. Nor were we ever accused of exercising good judgment by strictly adhering to common sense. By gaining experience through "on-the-job" training, we had a better chance of returning home. From the Army Guideline on Education, "Experience is the best teacher." Stated in grunt code: "That which does not kill you will make you smarter."

On one occasion, while on a "routine" night ambush patrol, our squad surprised an enemy patrol resulting in a horrendous firefight. We were a typical night patrol of ten men plus me, the medic. I was always the eleventh man. Although we were just a squad, we had a lot of firepower. Artillery support was immediately available to us, and air support was only minutes away. We called on infantry, artillery and air power to suppress the enemy fire. Fortunately, dusk turned into night, and darkness was our friend.

Unfortunately, the terrain consisted of a hard clay surface that lacked vegetation, which would have offered additional concealment. During the firefight, bullets were hitting all around us, so we started to "dig in" for protection. I was scared shitless and wondered how any of us were going to survive. But all of us did, to my relief and utter amazement. In this case, we surprised the enemy—advantage us. When the enemy surprised us, a bad day could quickly turn into a worse day. The dynamic of a firefight is genuinely unpredictable. During my tour of duty, I was in many firefights, where there were no casualties. On other occasions, a few rounds from a sniper killed one of our own.

Dig-in hardware typically included an entrenching tool. But an ambush patrol meant you traveled light so you could move quickly. Often, we left the entrenching tool behind. In a crisis, we could use a helmet to dig a small depression in the ground to lie in. Getting your body below the surface assured survivability in a firefight. On this particular night, we had neither entrenchment tools nor helmets. I hoped and prayed that no bullets would find any of us. Like all good soldiers, we learned from this patrol. Berets and soft hats were now out, and the unfashionable but practical steel-pots were back in. More on-the-job training!

I was very thankful for that lesson because a few weeks later, my helmet was knocked off my head by an enemy bullet. The steel pot was slightly altered, but my head remained intact. *Lucky me!* I never told my mom about that incident. Even though I never wore my beret after that memorable night incident, I still have it. Like my "dog tags," it was another cool war souvenir.

Chapter 9

Life in the Infantry or Adapting to the Boonies

Infantry is defined as a branch of the Army that engages in close range combat on foot. Completing an eight-week basic training course is the first task for every individual who enters the Army. Once completed, you are qualified to perform the basic job functions of a soldier in the infantry. Advanced Individual Training (AIT) enables a person to become specialized in some other military job. No matter how specialized a person becomes, however, he is still infantry at his core.

To all foot soldiers, the term "infantry" means heavily armed men hiking through the bush looking for bad guys to fight. Soldiers are called "grunts," and all patrols are referred to as "search-and-destroy." I suspect neither term needs further explanation. On some days, we traversed jungle, swamps, rice paddies and creeks. If we got lucky, our duty for the day consisted of providing security for a bridge or village, or for engineers performing a road clearing operation. This was usually uneventful activity, which we always welcomed, as opposed to a riskier search-and-destroy operation.

As a matter of routine before sundown, we would establish a safer position to rest and relax for the night. Besides trying to create a comfortable sleeping environment, we had to construct good fighting positions for troop security. These protective areas were called a Night Defensive Positions (NDP). We would buddy-up so two of us could dig a foxhole big enough for both of us to sleep in and possibly fight from. Sadly, the need to fight from our foxholes happened frequently.

Digging in for the night in a new NDP.

Looking back, I can't remember getting much sleep during my time in the bush. If we planned to stay in the same location for a few days, the foxholes we created were quite elaborate. We'd finish the task by placing trees, metal stakes or corrugated metal sheets across the top of our holes. Next, we'd carefully stack several layers of sandbags on the "roof" for protection from enemy mortars, rockets and rifle-propelled grenades (RPGs). Having a mortar hit a foxhole roof was frightening but not necessarily fatal. RPGs were greater threats. Man, we spent a lot of time digging holes in the bush.

Other devices deployed for protecting the NDP included concertina wire, hanging grenades, trip flares and strategically placed claymore mines. These instruments of enemy destruction were deployed around the entire perimeter. Feeling somewhat secure, then we'd finally chow down and sleep in shifts and take turns participating in night ambush patrols (AP) or perimeter listening posts (LP).

Staying in the bush for weeks at a time provided plenty of downtime during which we relaxed, played cards and wrote letters home. We endlessly cleaned our weapons and sharpened our bayonets and survival knives. Sometimes we'd wager on lodging a thrown hatchet into a rubber tree. I became quite efficient in my throwing technique and made a few bucks, which I usually lost playing gin rummy.

Frequently, soldiers would play "Stretch." In our version of the game, the object was to make the other player fall over from having to spread his legs too far apart. The players begin by facing each a few yards apart with their own heels and toes touching. We'd take turns trying to throw our bayonets into the ground outside the other player's feet. If the bayonet stuck, the other player had to move his foot to touch the bayonet while keeping his other foot in place. Play continued until one player fell or was unable to stretch far enough. This was a dangerous game as you can imagine, and I sometimes had to treat a bayonet injury to a foot. Dangerous times apparently called for dangerous amusements.

Playing stretch for entertainment and money.

Besides gin rummy, we often played a card game called "Hearts." I excelled at this game and eventually was awarded the informal title

"Hearts Champion of Vietnam." But there is more to this story. As a medic and therefore a natural risk-taker, while playing Hearts, I could more efficiently evaluate the risks and rewards of trading or keeping the Queen of Spades. So how did I become the Hearts Champion of Vietnam?

One afternoon, four of us were playing Hearts when one of the players asked, "What should we play for?" Someone suggested that instead of playing for money, we should play for the Hearts Championship of Vietnam. We all agreed and played for a few hours. By the end of the afternoon, I was not so graciously declared the winner. To this day, my title of Hearts Champion of Vietnam has never been challenged. Over the following decades, I have received many awards and recognitions, but Hearts Champion of Vietnam ranks near the top!

Most nights, right after chow, I'd usually set aside an hour to host "sick call." Soldiers would come to my area with a variety of ailments. My job was to treat the more mundane disorders and identify the more complex medical cases that required additional treatment. I'm convinced that I treated every ailment soldiers in combat can experience. Some of the rashes and other skin maladies didn't even have names.

Fortunately, I carried an extensive assortment of pills and ointments, so I could usually find a remedy that worked. Not very scientific, but practical. My responsibility was to keep as many soldiers as possible available for combat duty. Of course, those troops hoping for a reprieve from patrol duty didn't like my declaring them "fit for duty" because of some remedy from my medicine kit.

Our routine was simple—wake up in the morning, eat breakfast, exercise bowels and load up with ammo and C-rations. Early on, the squad leader received the day's patrol orders and shared insights about conditions we could expect to encounter. We started search-and-destroy patrols right after sunrise. Fully provisioned, and with the day's maps in hand, we started looking for bad guys. Late in the day, the captain would locate a nice spot to rest for the night, and our foxhole engineering talents would be put to the test again.

One time, we were in the bush for 119 straight days, which greatly improved my skills with a shovel and my aid bag. During this excursion, I often felt sorry for myself. If I had joined the navy, three hot meals a day and a cot every night would have been the norm. I still would have volunteered to be a corpsman, though, and with my luck would have been assigned to an infantry marine unit on the DMZ. In the final analysis, I was thankful for the misery I had come to know.

The platoon is getting briefed on the day's patrol orders.

In the field, it was common to clean up by bathing in a creek or taking a jungle shower. Washing in a creek is easy and refreshing. At times we'd spend an hour swimming or lounging in a big pool of water that we discovered on patrol. Somebody always had a bar of soap with them. What a treat! Sometimes, we bathed in our clothes and sometimes not, depending on the circumstances and relative safety.

Jungle showers, which I found ingenious, involved more work but were worth the effort. A soldier would take water from a utility water trailer slung into the perimeter by a Chinook helicopter. The water was potable and warm from the heat of the sun. A canvas bag would be filled with five gallons of water and then pulled by a rope to the top of a tripod. The bottom of the bag contained a spray nozzle that could be turned on or off. The three-step shower technique was so simple even a grunt medic could figure it out, sort of. Here's how it worked:

1) Open the spray nozzle and soak yourself, then turn off the nozzle.
2) Open the spray nozzle, lather up and turn off the nozzle.
3) Open the spray nozzle and rinse off.

After about six months, I learned to work the bag so the final rinse ended before I ran out of water. It was a nifty invention and worked great.

One time, it was my turn to take a shower in the hot sun. We were set up in the middle of a white sand perimeter, and I readied my bag of water on the tripod. Just as I completed the lather-up phase, enemy mortars began landing nearby. Without hesitation, everyone ran to the closest bunkers, me included. Unfortunately, my body was still covered in lather, and I executed a perfect naked slide through the sand into the bunker. I was proud of my technique but felt like a piece of sandpaper.

It was an awful experience, and I sat naked in the sandy bunker for fifteen minutes until the attack ended. Charlie must have been laughing his ass off as I refilled my shower bag to rinse off. I distinctly remember trying to get the coarse mixture of soap and sand out of bodily crevices I never knew existed.

My best living conditions in Vietnam were in a base camp tent. Is it any wonder that I've chosen to avoid camping for the rest of my life?

Infantry really means "becoming one with nature." Often, our day patrols covered five to ten kilometers, also known as "klicks." The modern Army utilizes a Global Positioning System to identify specific locations. We utilized the point man's ability to read a map and trust a compass for direction and to count and remember the number of steps taken between waypoints. Our point men were selected because they were the most observant tough guys and savvy to the ways of the enemy and the jungle. Many were woodsmen, and all were just plain rock-solid, good ol' country boys. They were covert, had nerves of steel and were always mindful of the area around them. They kept us alive and knowledgeable of our almost exact location of where we were on the map.

Most importantly, these brave warriors at the front of the column could spot an enemy combatant under very adverse conditions. They could smell the enemy cooking rice and fish from great distances. They could spot the slight movement of a sniper in a tree or sense the movement of an enemy soldier underground in a tunnel. I was always amazed by their special skills.

Church services in the bush. Note the jungle shower, which came in handy after Sunday services.

Depending on the terrain, we would sometimes patrol fifteen klicks in a day. It was downright brutal. I called all patrols "slogs." This was an apt term because we hiked through jungle, bamboo thickets, hot steamy tall grass, rice paddies, swamps, creeks and streams and perhaps a few hills and dales! We walked in chest-deep slimy water and through bamboo and brush.

When we came to a hill, our fearless leaders always wanted to know what was on top. As apprehensive draftees, we usually didn't care. We preferred the less curious approach. Since we were not offered a vote by the commander, though, we carried out his usual order and climbed that hill in search of the enemy and the summit. Sometimes, we'd stay at the top and dig in. Other times, we'd just stumble back down the hill.

I remember sitting on my steel pot one night with my legs crossed in front of me. I fell asleep and started snoring, which was a big no-no. The high decibel volume of a snore or a snort could give our location away to the enemy. The soldier next to me pushed me on the shoulder, and I fell over like a bowling pin. My legs had fallen asleep, and I struggled to stretch them out. Thank God, no VC heard the commotion, otherwise, our perfectly peaceful ambush patrol would have turned into another bad night.

In spite of what you may think, I found infantry soldiers to be pretty darn smart. Although we were all fearful, no one showed fear. We knew we could rely on each other to handle any adversity. While we always followed orders, we did, at times, question their rationale.

The combat strategy in Vietnam was, "Find the enemy, engage the enemy, kill as many as possible and then withdraw to fight another day." Military and political leaders assumed that a high enemy body count would eventually cause the VC and NVA to surrender. They believed Ho Chi Minh and his army couldn't possibly sustain such losses and would surely lose their will to fight. Well, that philosophy probably looked good on paper but didn't reflect reality. Losing the will to fight? WRONG!

I concede that VC (local) units were less skilled and not as well-equipped or trained as the NVA (regular army) units. We knew whenever we got into a firefight with the NVA, they always stuck around until the proverbial "last dog was hung." Their combat determination was complete and unwavering. They believed in their mission to reunite the North with the South and would not be deterred in their resolve.

As a result, our unit fought many battles in the same territory, but we always withdrew and surrendered the land back to the enemy. Then we'd repeat this tactic. And then do it again. To all of us "ground-pounders," it seemed more logical after seizing territory to hold it. Eventually, then, we'd be able to push the VC and NVA totally out of Vietnam. That approach had been quite effective in WWI and WWII, and to some extent, it worked in the Korean Conflict. But this approach in Vietnam was not to be. There was no political will to commit the number of soldiers necessary to make that happen.

Unfortunately, this approach to war led to many additional casualties because we fought for the same turf again and again. The enemy did not surrender, and significant progress on our part was at best allusive. We all knew that such a seize-and-withdraw strategy was flawed. If we were going to fight, let us win the battle and eventually declare victory at the end of the war.

The military strategy we were asked to execute was frustrating, to say the least. We also knew the enemy body count was often inflated to satisfy goals established by Washington bureaucrats. While we were aware of how many soldiers we lost, we never accurately knew how many the enemy had lost. After a battle, the enemy efficiently removed the dead bodies of comrade soldiers from the battlefield. This interfered with our ability to get an accurate count. Maybe we killed the same enemy soldiers repeatedly!

Counting bodies was always difficult, but combat soldiers do not set policy. Such matters were, as they say, "well above our pay grade." Like all good grunts, we learned to suffer in relative silence and simply went about our routine, which included counting the days until we'd go home.

Machetes were as essential to fighting the jungle as rifles were to fighting the enemy. On occasion, they were as crucial for the point man as his rifle. That unfortunate soul had to cut paths through the jungle for the rest of the column to walk through. The rule was to avoid footpaths and trails because such easy walking paths could mean injury or death from booby traps and snipers.

Jungle travel was taxing physically and mentally. Patrolling in the jungle would kick the hell out of you, plain and simple. The jungle was no tropical paradise—it was hot, humid and infested with savage bugs and reptiles. Swarms of mosquitos were often as thick as the jungle itself. At night they ferociously attacked with even more cunning, seeming to plan and execute their insect assaults with great precision. Insect repellant left our skin with an oily burning sensation and was not effective at all.

I am from Minnesota, where mosquitos are abundant and very persistent. I thought the Minnesota strains were the biggest pests in the world—descendants of vampires, it seemed. But the "back home skitters" couldn't compete with their Nam cousins. To put the size of the Vietnam mosquitos in perspective, I generally tell people, "The mosquitoes in Vietnam were so big they could stand flat-footed and make love to a turkey." Just one more reason why we were happy to leave Vietnam.

Like all infantry soldiers, we were constantly being pushed beyond our personal limits. We had no choice but to endure. Completing the mission, even when the terrain seemed impossible to navigate, was a high priority. Quitting was not an option.

I have searing memories of heat and fatigue. While heatstroke was rare, heat exhaustion was not. Every soldier carried two canteens, but as the medic, I carried four. Water and salt tablets were standard treatment for overexertion. My job was to make sure everyone stayed hydrated. If we came across a stream and our canteens were empty, we'd fill them up. I'd hand out iodine tablets to purify the water. One time, the water was so putrid I added six tablets to each canteen. The liquid passed for water, and I knew it was potable, but it still tasted like squirrel piss. But, what the heck, we re-hydrated, and no one came down with hepatitis. Lucky us! Just one more thing to tell the grandkids someday.

Refilling canteens while on patrol. As the medic, I issued iodine tablets for each canteen to kill hostile bacteria and make the water safe to drink.

Jungle trails were prime locations for the enemy to set up ambushes. The VC knew that exhausted American GIs would usually take the path of least resistance. Some did and paid the price. But our officers and NCOs knew the risks associated with trails and proved to us the benefits of taking the tougher path. I developed some slogans to help me remember this important doctrine.

"Chop the bush and save your tush!"

"Hike the grass and save your ass."

"Stay off the trail to avoid the hail... of bullets."

I know these catchphrases were dumb, but they served as reminders of the consequences. Besides, walking on a patrol can be boring, with ample opportunity for the mind to wander. Stay focused, stay alert and don't be bored—all at the same time. Therein lies the conflict. This is how it went in the infantry.

I have witnessed plenty of injuries when this fundamental "stay focused" rule was ignored. I treated soldiers who stepped into pits containing punji sticks, a weapon used by the Viet Cong as a booby trap. Punji sticks were thin, sharpened stakes of bamboo or wood placed at an angle in a pit where US troops were likely to be passing. Although stepping into a punji pit did extensive damage and inflicted a great deal of pain, the wounds were never fatal. Most often, the puncture wounds ran deep, and some of the cuts were so jagged it was difficult to stop the bleeding. I usually washed out the wound, poured ample amounts of Merthiolate on the puncture and then tightly applied compression bandages. As the final step, I'd cover these nasty wounds with Ace elastic wraps to hold it all together. Ace wraps were a medic's best "battle dressing" friend.

Frequently, the Viet Cong would dip the punji stick tips in human feces to infect the wound. Toxicity was my biggest worry, so it was important to quickly get the soldier started on antibiotics. This meant calling for a "dust-off" to evacuate the soldier, which slowed down the patrol and revealed our location to the enemy. That was precisely what the enemy wanted so they could stage follow-up sniper attacks. Eventually, we became much more skilled at identifying and avoiding booby traps before they could inflict harm.

I vividly remember the nasty, invasive red clay, the endless mud, and the creepy, crawling things that silently slithered off branches onto my body. I used lit cigarettes to burn leeches off my body. Nasty! The stings of fire ants were immensely painful. Scorpions were abundant and very toxic but not deadly, as portrayed in the movies.

Getting stung by a scorpion was like getting stung by a bee and was dangerous only if a soldier was allergic to the venom. Many of my troopers had encounters with scorpions and bees, but none proved fatal. I administered an antihistamine to the afflicted.

You couldn't beat the bush very long without developing a constant watchfulness for snakes on branches above your head or in the water. I crossed paths with many snakes while on patrol or sleeping in my bunker. Every snake I encountered was poisonous or a constrictor that could crush your bones. Most of us were more afraid of snakes than of the VC. As a rule, I slept with one eye open for Charlie and one eye open for snakes and scorpions, which meant I hardly slept at all.

I was fortunate to never get bitten or constricted. Some soldiers in my charge, however, were not so lucky. I had to use my snake bite kit and on-the-job training to treat the unlucky and evacuate them to get anti-venom serum.

Since the infantry is the backbone of the Army, we felt a special pride. Generally, we were well-supplied. We were given a change of clothes once a week whether we needed fresh ones or not. We never wore underwear because that led to crotch rot. We slept in the mud or on an air mattress if we could find one.

During the monsoon season, staying dry was a real challenge. We all carried ponchos, which would keep out the rain but also kept in the heat and made you feel like you were trapped in a personal sauna. Ponchos also made a lot of noise when you were moving through the bush. We never wore ponchos on nighttime ambush patrol, where stealth was key to survival. While it was uncomfortable to be rained on, it was much safer to suck it up and get wet.

Soldiers universally agree that the worse thing about the monsoon season was lighting a cigarette. That was the one indulgence freely afforded us, even though it was bad for our health. But so were bullets! I found it best to carry a towel, so during a major downpour, I could still cover my head and light my cig.

Most of us never smoked before we joined the infantry, but each box of C-Rations contained a small individual packet with four cigarettes. Most of us quickly gave into curiosity and took up smoking. There was no surgeon general warning about the health hazards clearly stamped on each pack of cigs, just as there was no surgeon general warning against the hazards of warfare stamped on our ammo.

Smoking helped us pass the time, relax and otherwise distract our unpretentious minds from the realities of our circumstances. It was easy to smoke because once a week our supply chopper would bring clean clothes, ammo, food supplies and cases of cigarettes. If you wanted to smoke, the US government provided free cigarettes for every soldier in a combat unit. No charge, no fee, no worries and certainly no rational thinking. I think everyone took up the habit except for our two Latter-Day Saints medics.

Cigarettes also served as barter with the local camp followers, who always seemed to know exactly where we were in the middle of the jungle. While these followers were most likely VC spies, they did offer us sodas, trinkets and other services.

As for the big picture, here's how the infantry worked. Most of the time, the general would gather his senior staff and identify an area that needed our attention. Then they'd provide helicopters to transport us to the identified site hoping it would be full of hostiles. The landing zone (LZ) is where the patrol began. Usually, the LZ was free of enemy combatants, but not always. Too frequently, VC or NVA fighters were in ambush.

A "hot LZ," which meant that hostiles were engaged where we planned to land, was especially terrifying. We couldn't wait to get on the ground because the choppers were large targets, and we felt like ducks in a shooting gallery. I was always amazed that more soldiers were not killed or wounded during chopper insertions and extractions. But one of the loneliest feelings I ever had was watching my helicopter transport leaving a hot LZ after dropping me off. Even with a hundred other warriors, I still felt very alone.

We spent a lot of time shuttling around the jungles and villages of Vietnam. We were part of the new Army air mobile infantry. "Air mobile" meant we would fly to remote areas via helicopters, and "infantry" meant we would recon or patrol large areas on foot. Sometimes we were relocated every few days. As a mode of transportation, I preferred the helicopter over a truck or tracked vehicle. We could move easier, carry our necessary supplies and start the mission sooner.

In choppers, we flew fast just above the trees. Fast-moving choppers are more difficult to target, and in the air, we didn't have to worry about land mines blowing up a truck or a tank. I was inserted by helicopter into battle areas so many times it became routine, but not necessarily uneventful. I made so many air assaults that the Army gave me an Air Medal. The citation stated I had made twenty-five air assaults. I spent a lot of time in Huey helicopters. These craft were more than transports—they were lifesavers.

An infantry company is made up of three rifle platoons and a headquarters platoon. Usually, we were short replacement soldiers, which kept us well understrength during my tour. A full complement infantry company usually consists of one hundred and fifty soldiers. In Vietnam, our company was lucky to muster ninety-five to one hundred and ten soldiers for field operations, which made the job a lot harder and patrolling more dangerous. The Army clearly believed there was safety in numbers. More soldiers, more firepower and more damage inflicted on the enemy, not us.

Jungle warfare is not safe. As a result, our frequent engagements and casualties, when combined with mandatory soldier rotations, made it almost impossible to maintain a full complement of soldiers. We sure as hell did not want to have anybody extend their tour in Vietnam because we didn't have enough soldiers. My guess is that the same situation occurred in all infantry units regardless of the war or battle operations. Complaining about workforce shortages was clearly the duty of every grunt.

Each platoon was made up of three squads, each comprised of ten soldiers. Each soldier had different skill sets and weapons. A 2nd lieutenant and a staff sergeant commanded our infantry line platoon. A radio operator (RTO) and a medic rounded out the so-called non-combatant cadre. As a medic, I was not expected to engage in the firefights, but I did when necessary. I felt more secure with my weapon close at hand, though my M-16 rifle was a distraction when treating a casualty. I lost an M-16 in one firefight, but that's another story.

Each squad was led by a sergeant and included several riflemen with M-16s, a sniper with an M-14, one M-60 machine gunner and his assistant, a grenadier with an M-79, and an M-72 Light Anti-Tank Weapon called the LAW. The medic assigned to each platoon was responsible for the health and welfare of every soldier in the platoon. From head colds to sucking chest wounds, we handled it all.

The headquarters platoon medic was called the senior medic and was responsible for the overall medical well-being of all soldiers in the company. The senior medic was also in charge of the three-line platoon medics. I eventually achieved that status, which meant more responsibility for an additional forty dollars per month.

Every day, I'd give each soldier in my unit salt tablets to prevent heat exhaustion and cramps. Once a week, I'd dole out malaria tablets. I guess these pills were effective because none of my guys came down with malaria. I attributed that success to either good science or simply no one being attacked by a disease-carrying mosquito. Probably the science.

On occasion, the battalion physician would order the medics to perform a "short arm" inspection, which meant we had to examine every soldier for evidence of venereal disease. It doesn't take much explanation to identify which "short arm" was to be inspected. This was a humbling experience for both the examinee and the medic examiner. The presence of this awful condition was always painfully obvious.

I remember that most daytime search-and-destroy patrols were platoon-size. If Army intelligence identified a significant enemy concentration in an area, a company-size or even an occasional battalion-size patrol was sent out.

Leaving the safety of the perimeter to begin the day's patrol was anything but routine. You had to be alert to booby traps set during the night or an ambush that could start your day in a bad way. At first light, we always knew to expect the unexpected. Because food is essential for sustaining happy soldiers, we usually got a hot breakfast before starting our daily routine sweep. The weather was always hot and humid. Our clothes would be soaked in sweat even before starting our patrol. I still remember the loud sounds of magazines being loaded into the M-16s and the high-velocity rounds being chambered as we exited the safety of the perimeter through the concertina wire. Those sounds quickly changed the mood, shifting our mindset to war. We were now ready for the unexpected.

I also remember the sounds of nature, which provided guidance on how our daily adventure was to proceed. If the birds were chirping, it was a good thing. If the baboons were hollering, it was not a good thing—something was obviously disturbing their routine. Maybe just the fuss we were making. We hoped so.

In the bush, danger was a constant companion, and we were always ready to do battle. My anxiety worked overtime the whole year I was in Vietnam. Once I got out of the Army and back onto a college campus, it took a long time to de-escalate emotionally. At least as a civilian, I didn't need my combat armament or aid bag to deal with unsavory professors or war protestors.

The job of the infantry in a war zone was to conduct reconnaissance-in-force operations (RIFs). This meant sending out patrols to gather intelligence about enemy concentrations and movements. The stated mission objective was "to survey a given geographical area, make contact and kill the enemy." So, war is really about capturing territory on a short-term basis and counting corpses.

I had a tough time applying logic to this objective. It seemed to me that the generals were obsessed with the "enemy body count" objective, but the rank and file soldiers were not so enthusiastic about it. Maybe this goal was less appealing to the grunts because we had to endure the firefights and battles to achieve that enemy body count. The firefights were when reality set in, the fun ended, and life-altering personal hardships began. That's war for you.

The daily body count reports combined with our own escalating casualty figures added fuel to the fire of domestic anti-war protests.

It seemed to me that the solution to ending these protests was quite simple—either quit reporting the body counts or end the war.

But this was a different kind of war being fought under new pretexts and with new technology for reporting on it. Journalists covering the Vietnam War took advantage of this new technology and could report on a battle right after it happened. There were no secrets after the fact. The national media brought the war into the homes of our parents and loved ones during the nightly news, and the public didn't like what they were seeing. As a result, protests back home grew in frequency and intensity.

As combat participants, we grunts were not immune from the questions being raised by journalists who were occasionally embedded with us. Reporters queried us about the seriousness of our battles and asked how we thought our government was going to resolve this conflict in Vietnam. These were difficult questions for hot, sweaty, exhausted soldiers who were more interested in getting better food and a pack of Kool-Aid to spice up the contents of their canteens. It was not easy to function under such political chaos and civilian disenchantment. Nevertheless, we continued to bravely fight the enemy when engaged.

Out of necessity, we soldiers tried to make life less complex. Rather than focus on the uncertainty of public discontent and governmental chaos, we looked out for each other. The special bond between soldiers was unbreakable. To a man, we just wanted to help each other complete our tour and get back home in one piece.

The essential tools for an infantry soldier include a rifle, Claymore mines, hand grenades, an entrenching tool (small shovel), a machete, an air mattress, canteens, a large battle dressing, ammo, some C-rations and a P-38 (explained later.) Next to his rifle, the P-38 was the second most important instrument for a grunt.

Because an army moves on its stomach, infantry soldiers were always thinking about food. We could usually count on getting at least one hot meal a day, which was prepared by cooks back at base camp and flown to our jungle location by chopper. The food was served out of field cans supposedly designed to keep the contents hot. Sometimes it was hot, but most times it was not. Even so, it was food, and I always ate everything offered.

The other two meals each day were C-rations. We called them C-rats for obvious reasons. We believed most of these "yummy meals" were left over from WWII. Hey, the C-rats passed for nutrition, and since a soldier is always hungry, he'll eat anything. My favorite was the B-3 unit, which was ham and lima beans for the main course.

Each C-ration box included an entree, fruit, chocolate, coffee and cigarettes. The box also contained a small packet of toilet paper. To give context to this packet, I should call it a "swath of toilet paper." When put to the test, it was barely enough to clean your nose and not nearly enough to address the other body part that required attention due to a condition frequently remedied in other ways.

So, what is a P-38? One thing for sure, it was not an airplane. Rather, it was an instrument as important and often more practical than a bar of soap. It was an item to be cherished and kept on your person in a safe place. It was always with you and deployed as frequently as possible. You learned to use it in a variety of ways, including picking your teeth or cleaning mud from your weapon or boots. A P-38 was a small, angular piece of sharpened steel used to open the cans in your C-rats.

Once opened and ready for consumption, these C-rat meals relied heavily on generous doses of Louisiana Hot Sauce. This spicy condiment enhanced the food's flavor and, in some respects, made it edible. If a grunt was lucky, he had access to a little plastic explosive (C-4) to heat up the rations. A hot meal was always better, as was hot coffee.

C-4 was tricky to use but highly effective. It would only explode if it applied kinetic force to the burning fuel. That is what a blasting cap does to the C-4. But we were smart soldiers and avoided stomping on the burning fuel at all costs. I remember being amazed at how ingenious soldiers can be—and how much better food tasted hot.

Cooking up a hot lunch using C-4 as the fuel source. Just don't stomp on it or it will go boom!

Chapter 10

Duties of a Combat Medic

The GO ARMY website states, "While there are other health care positions available in the Army, you'd be hard-pressed to find a military occupational specialty (MOS) as exciting (and dangerous) as that of the combat medic."

The website goes on to explain, "While any enlistee with the willingness and aptitude can become a combat medic, ideally these candidates will possess strong communication skills, empathy, attention to detail, an interest in the sciences (especially biology and anatomy) and the ability to handle lots of stress under the most trying of circumstances."

Although I just learned of this description, I personally can attest that all of this is true. Upon further reflection, that is exactly how I viewed myself.

According to Army recruitment documents, the important characteristics possessed by a combat medic are compassion, a strong resolve to help others and being a risk-taker. Everything we did in Vietnam involved risks. Some were just bigger than others.

I tried to consistently express compassion through my actions and always offered words of comfort to the wounded. Sometimes, the circumstances were extremely distressing, and my words fell on lifeless ears. Soldiers were trained to fight, and medics were trained to put broken soldiers back together. Out of necessity, I learned to do my job and move on. I also discovered my brothers-in-arms were glad to have me on patrol with them. None of us wanted to get shot or become a combat injury, but we all knew that was a possibility.

The Army was good at sending troops on patrol and putting us in the bullseye of the VC or NVA. Going into harm's way was part of our job descriptions. I've been told there was comfort in knowing a medic was on patrol to render aid should the unimaginable happen. To an infantry soldier, comfort is knowing the "Doc" has your back. Comfort to a medic was knowing my brothers always had mine.

Whenever you faithfully execute the duties of your job in a firefight, other participants and witnesses occasionally conclude you were brave and courageous. To me, this rationale is as peculiar as war itself. Regardless of the assigned job, soldiers do what they are supposed to do. No big debate with yourself. No pre-conceived plan. No thoughts of flag or country. No reflections on patriotism or the evils of communism. I found it curious that the Army gives medals for simply doing what needed to be done.

Medals? I've gotten some. I must admit I'm proud of these recognitions because they remind me that a half-century ago, my commanders thought I did the best job I could do. I always thought I was just in the right place at the wrong time.

Medics served an important role with the infantry. Within a typical combat unit, medics functioned as a member of an infantry platoon until the point that a comrade was wounded. The Vietnam War was the first time medics were directly embedded into infantry units. Having a medic participate with very small units on patrol was a new Army protocol specifically designed to save lives. The goal was to render aid very soon after a battle injury occurred. This new protocol saved many lives that would have most likely have been lost in previous wars.

Vietnam was also the first time that medics carried firearms and other fighting instruments like grenades in combat. Red crosses on helmets and armbands were no longer worn. Unlike previous wars in which medics were respected by both sides, Vietnam War medics were targeted for injury or death by the enemy. The only way an observant enemy combatant could tell I was a medic was by the aid bag I carried.

The author is combat-ready with M-16 and aid bag. We all wore the government-issued "tailored" uniform.

The VC and NVA were paid a five-hundred-dollar bounty for killing an officer, the Radio Transmission Operator (RTO) or a medic. They believed that if the medic was killed, the other American soldiers would not be willing to fight or give chase and would withdraw from the firefight. Although this thinking was false, it was in every medic's best interest to blend in with the other soldiers. I believed it was critical to my survival. I unequivocally knew, however, that my presence on patrols provided comfort and added to the psychological well-being of the soldiers in my unit. They treated me with respect and deep trust.

Carl Bradfield made the following observations about the importance of combat medics in his book *The Blue Spaders of Vietnam*, published in 1992. Bradfield spent a year as a rifleman in the 1/26th Regiment of the 1st Infantry Division in Vietnam, which was my outfit.

Bradfield wrote, "I would like to say something about the medics before I forget. Though I mentioned some in previous chapters, enough cannot be said in praise of those men. If there were any heroes who emerged out of the war, it was the medics. Every man in combat came to appreciate the guys known as 'Doc.' Their lives were as miserable as ours, and they had the same odds of life and death. Yet, their value to the wounded was immeasurable. Many of them hadn't had much more training in combat first aid than we had. They went through a training course and emerged with great responsibility, more than should've been placed on them. In war, they were expected to have the answer to every bloody situation."

Besides treating routine maladies and combat injuries, medics occasionally filled the role of mental health therapist. Soldiers felt comfortable around us and believed we could solve any problem, be it physical or mental, regardless of the complexity. I had men share their most personal problems with me. By nature, most medics are compassionate and good listeners. In response, my troops trusted me.

Even though in combat I was full of fear and apprehension, I was honored to play an important role during those times I rendered aid, including mental health services. Many soldiers had to deal with some very heavy mental and emotional issues—a death in the family, drug problems, the embarrassment and potential military discipline associated with self-inflicted injury or getting a venereal disease, to name a few.

Some guys had received Dear John letters while in Vietnam, which left them confused and angry. These letters were direct shots to the heart and very hard to accept by combat-hardened men in the field with plenty of time on their hands. It was natural for these grunts to think the worst and feel angry. This combination could be as lethal as combat itself because it could lead a soldier to do stupid things and make unhealthy decisions. When you add combat conditions to a ten-thousand-mile separation, you can have a major psychological disaster on your hands.

Imagine a soldier who is a pretty intelligent and creative person. But at the same time, he was inexperienced in love, let alone relationships. I was always the go-to guy for support in these cases because I was the medic and two years older than most of the 11Bs. It was easier to discuss such personal situations with me than, let's say, the first sergeant or captain. I was never trained in mental health support and no more prepared to offer worldly advice or therapeutic solutions than the company demolition man (also known as the explosives expert) whose solution to every problem was to use more explosives and make a bigger bang!

Somehow, because I was the medic, these distraught young men shared their most intimate secrets with me as if I were their chaplain or psychologist. Of course, I was a good listener, and I genuinely wanted to fix every condition that affected the well-being of my troops. After all, I had successfully completed my medical training, where I learned that the most important lesson is to exhibit confidence when rendering advice.

Sometimes my advice was very creative. Other times I suspect it was downright stupid. Creative or stupid often reflected the problems presented to me, so they warranted a like response.

I recall when one of my guys got a Dear John letter from his wife. His mother had recently died, so he had decided to ask his now-widowed father to look after his young wife while he was in Vietnam. In her correspondence, she told her soldier husband that she wanted a divorce so she could marry his father. *Now, that was heavy!* He was extraordinarily upset. Even I became judgmental and got pissed off. From a medical perspective, I believed this trooper was incapable of discharging his duties as a rifleman because of the emotional distress. But we were in the field, and it was getting dark. So, what to do? It was too late to call for a helicopter to transport him to the rear for a proper mental health evaluation.

Out of options, I thought about taking him to the company first sergeant, who was affectionately known as "Top," as in the top enlisted man. Since Top had always portrayed himself as "all-wise and knowing," certainly he would have advice for this thorny problem. But the life stories Top frequently shared with me had left the impression that Top really wasn't equipped for this challenge.

I thought about telling this kid he should just go home and kill his daddy because he obviously needed killing. But that fantasy soon passed. I was not coming up with any practical advice, so I chose instead to listen… and listen… and listen to him vent. I offered an occasional "Yup" and "Wow, that really sucks."

About four hours later, the soldier ran out of words and came to his own conclusion that she just wasn't worth the sweat of his balls and that his daddy was an asshole. I agreed and supported his decision to change his ten-thousand-dollar life insurance beneficiary to his sister.

By the next morning, my young ward was in a much better frame of mind and deemed ready for another day on patrol. The soldier completed his tour and seemed perfectly normal when he left the unit. However, the definition of normal was clearly left to one's own imagination. I have always wondered about the rest of his story.

Finally, I hunkered down in my foxhole to get some sleep. As I lay there waiting for the sweet dreams to arrive (they never did in a combat zone,) I thought to myself, *I am now a seasoned veteran at all things medical because I believe I've developed the expertise to call myself an untrained but skilled closet therapist. Hell, at least I'm gaining more experience on this front every week.*

I wondered if a guy could make money on the outside with such highly developed skills.

The bottom line: A medic must be a quick thinker, creative problem solver and an extremely patient listener. While in Vietnam, I had to deal with everything imaginable. I learned some problems were bigger than others, but the solutions were often the same. Whether the problems were mental or physical, it was necessary to develop a plan and execute—to be decisive and do what needs to be done. After all, in the bush, who you gonna call?

Just like the expression, "There are no atheists in a foxhole," I can attest there are no psychologists in the jungle except for us "closet therapists." I have always felt deeply privileged to be trusted so completely by these hardened combat veterans. I cherish their bestowed trust and confidence to this day.

In Vietnam, combat medics raised the survivability rate on the battlefield to 92 percent. The development of advanced field treatment techniques and equipment, combined with the extensive use of medevac helicopters (dust-offs,) allowed thousands of young men to return home who in previous wars would have died.

Thanks to mobile air support in Vietnam, it was possible for a wounded soldier to reach a hospital within two hours. Unfortunately, the perils of nighttime extractions frequently took longer. This enhanced capability was a far cry from World War I, the first industrialized war, when the journey from the trenches to the field hospital could take between twelve and forty-eight hours.

The term "combat medic" perfectly described my job in an infantry unit. The contents of my aid bag included: five morphine syrettes, one bottle of saline solution, one bottle of lump albumin, malaria pills, iodine, salt tablets, compress battle dressings, some petroleum gauze dressings for sucking chest wounds, Ace wraps, two pneumatic splints (one leg and one arm), a soft litter, a stethoscope, clamps, sutures, tourniquets, and an assortment of pills and ointments. I also carried a bottle of Merthiolate, a highly effective disinfectant for cleaning cuts, scrapes and battle wounds. My aid bag weighed about ten pounds. In addition, I carried a rope, an M-16, a bayonet, six magazines for my rifle, one Claymore mine, two hand grenades, one flashlight complete with colored filters, and four canteens.

As in previous wars, many medics were conscientious objectors. These were and still are solid citizens who wanted to serve but objected to carrying a weapon or taking someone's life. My company had four medics, and two of them were COs—great and capable guys who were fearless. They did their job well and put themselves in harm's way to help wounded soldiers. I thought highly of their commitment to their troops and their apparent disregard for their own safety. Furthermore, they did not refuse to be drafted or go to Canada to avoid the draft. They stood tall and accepted their fate along with the rest of us. They went on patrols and sweeps just like everyone else. I can't imagine what it must have been like to be the subject of incoming hostile enemy fire without the ability to reciprocate.

On the other hand, I had no ethical issues about carrying an M-16 or any other Army-issued weapons of deterrence and destruction. I felt strongly about defending myself and protecting wounded soldiers in my care.

During one firefight, I lost my M-16 because I couldn't carry my rifle and my casualty at the same time. When I returned to our base camp at Quan Loi, I went to the supply sergeant and asked for another M-16 to replace the one I abandoned. In typical Army fashion, he read me the riot act. He even made references to the marital status of my parents when I was born by calling me a bastard. He snarled and yelled that I lacked respect for him and our taxpayer-provided government property.

By the end of his tirade, he made it clear he would not issue me a replacement M-16. He opted instead to issue me a .45 caliber pistol, complete with holster, utility belt and a box of bullets. Knowing I couldn't hit shit with the pistol, I insisted on being given two additional hand grenades to accompany the two I already carried. Having four grenades made me feel much more confident than possessing just two grenades and a pistol. Grenades were outstanding instruments for protection and an effective deterrent to anyone who displayed hostile intent. They were much more efficient than the pistol.

As a matter of full disclosure, I only used hand grenades as "defensive weapons," which I believed to be consistent with the Geneva Convention.

Eventually, and after several grenade resupply missions from the supply armament sergeant, he once again trusted me enough to replace my lost M-16. He did mumble something like, "For a medic, you sure go through a lot of hand grenades." Interestingly, I did not have to give up my sidearm or my extra two hand grenades to get the M-16. My instruments of defense and I were now one. Besides, I believed it was much better for the enemy to need the services of his medic than for my brothers to need my services.

In Vietnam, unlike today's soldiers, none of us in the straight-leg infantry wore personal body armor. In fact, it wasn't available to regular combat soldiers until the Iraq War. This evolution in protection, along with the Kevlar helmet, was practical and necessary. These utility devices have saved a lot of lives and dramatically reduced injuries.

Those of us who served in Vietnam wore a helmet we affectionately called a steel pot. Its ability to protect your head was obvious, but it also served as a dandy device for holding water for a shave or washing your socks. WWII-style flak jackets were worn by personnel in mechanized or mobile units because they were frequently attacked by enemy rockets, RPGs and heavy mortars that could send a lot of nasty shrapnel your way. However, these old-style navy flak jackets were not nearly as effective as today's body armor. Massive injuries still occurred. While they did offer minimal protection, many were frequently cast aside because they were hot and bulky. Fortunately, during my time of tour, the NVA didn't shoot many RPGs at us. They didn't want to waste their precious RPGs on straight-leg grunts.

Chapter 11

Landing Zones

Mobile air-assaults were never fun and seldom routine. They are like trying to cross the ocean in a dingy with a 5 HP outboard. Either you make it, or you become fish fodder. The problem with a landing zone (LZ) is you must land in them at the beginning of the mission and exit from them once the mission has been completed. There was never such thing as a safe landing zone. Some were merely less risky.

Sometimes, when you make it to the LZ and exit the chopper, you wish you hadn't. Some chopper flights are like riding on a roller coaster and Tilt-A-Whirl at the same time. It's amazing that soldiers did not routinely fall out of these hearty transports.

Chopper rides were always noisy with hot wind blowing through the cabin. There were no doors on the helicopter, only two-door gunners, each armed with an M-60 machine gun mounted on a sling. One of these machine guns was strapped to each side of the craft. The door gun operators were expert marksmen and added significant firepower to the mobile unit. It made us feel more comfortable in our low altitude travel adventures.

Unfortunately, the Huey helicopter and the soldiers they carried made excellent targets, so I was always on edge when flying on a combat mission. Conversely, this newly developed air-assault technique greatly expanded the sphere of military operations. Air-assaults also enabled a sizable military force to be deployed in an area of operation in a very short period. Safety in numbers is a good thing.

The idea was to bring the fight to the enemy. The goal was to deploy an overwhelmingly superior US force to a hostile area, thereby surprising and trapping the enemy. This approach was designed to inflict maximum damage on an unsuspecting enemy and obtain a high enemy body count. The US Army had firepower superiority over the enemy, so the objective was to decimate the Viet Cong or NVA combat capability and reduce the enemy's willingness to fight. Most of the time, this approach to combat worked extremely well. Sometimes, not so much.

Occasionally, it was evident that the LZ was not well-researched or prepped for landing. In other words, the hazards weren't clearly identified and communicated to the force participating in the assault. Too often, it seemed that the only criteria for locating the LZ was, "Is it big enough for five choppers to land at one time?" Never mind the viability or condition of the selected LZ site.

A lot of guesswork and hope went into the LZ decision-picking process. After our combat unit was inserted by chopper, we had plenty of time to be amazed. Little questions would make their way into your minds, like: "Is there water under the tall grass covering the LZ? How deep do you think it is?" The strategy often seemed to be, "Oh well, guess we'll just drop the troops into the unknown and let them find out if there's water there."

I remember one insertion into a "hot" LZ. In this context, "hot" is an expression used to describe the intensity of the enemy fire and the volume of mortars targeting our point of insertion. Unfortunately, in this insertion, the enemy was set up in the wood line about two hundred yards from us. With bullets zinging around us and RPGs crisscrossing the sky, our chopper pilot hovered and loudly yelled for us to get out. As an officer and a very smart man, he recognized danger. No sense sticking around to chitchat any longer than necessary. I always thought the pilots and crew of these capable flight vehicles were extraordinarily brave to just hover like a sitting duck while we exited the craft under covering fire.

A flight of Huey's arriving to take us out on another company-sized air assault.

It soon became apparent, however, that the chopper was not going to return us to the safety of our base. It also became obvious that the pilot was not going to touch the ground. We followed his anxious command to "EXIT THE AIRCRAFT, NOW!"

We hurriedly jumped ten feet into the tall grass and water. Now that was a surprise, and thank God, the water was only a few feet deep and broke our fall. The grass gave us some concealment. *Wow, that sure was fun! Welcome to life in the new mobile Army.* Like a lot of things I did in Vietnam, I immediately scratched that experience off my bucket list.

Soon enough, we exited our watery death trap and moved to drier ground and better cover. The best part? No one was wounded, although a few soldiers suffered minor sprains and pains. I remember how difficult it was to move out of the grass and water. This wet, tall, grassy environment was blistering and humid, and the field was full of mud, which desperately tried to hold us in place. The landing site must have once been a very productive rice paddy. *Welcome to LZ Charley!*

We couldn't wait to get back to our base camp to look up the guy who planned that operation. Oh well, even though it was my first hot LZ experience, I knew it wasn't going to be the last. For what it's worth, I never did find the guy who picked that spot to land.

On another occasion, we completed our mission, and it was time for extraction. Even though we patrolled the area for only a few days, we had engaged the enemy in numerous small firefights. Our mission had evolved into constant harassing fire by both sides. Fortunately, our heavy artillery salvos, followed up by bombers and gunships, did a great job destroying the enemy base camp we had stumbled upon. Finding an enemy base camp was a big deal, and we were always able to put a physical and psychological "hurt" on the enemy. Besides generating a body count for the general, we seized large amounts of supplies and ammunition.

The hilly terrain made it a challenge to get to our pickup zone. When we finally arrived, the ground was littered with numerous tree stumps and unexploded ordnance called butterfly bombs. The zone was large enough for five choppers to come in at one time so we could be extracted more quickly.

As we prepared to board our assigned Huey, we came under attack once again. We responded immediately, overwhelming the VC with enough firepower to temporarily suppress the attack. Taking advantage of a lull in the action, we quickly loaded the choppers to depart. In our haste to exit, we overloaded some of the Hueys, pushing them beyond their weight capacity. This made it exceedingly difficult to lift off.

That day, I learned another new lesson. Hostile incoming gunfire is a sure way to dismiss capacity limits and air safety in the hope of getting the hell out of there! The lack of volunteers to remain behind required the pilots to fully utilize their flying skills. No one wanted to hang around.

So, there we were, hugging our air taxi, waiting for the up, up and away moment. As I said, it was a very hot day with high humidity, and we were attempting to leave from a hilltop about two thousand feet high, which complicated the lift-off because of thinner air. I'm sure the Army manual indicated taking off in thin air with an overweight load was the worst possible condition. Our gutsy masters of the craft pushed the engine beyond its point of maximum capability. I remember the jet engine turbine making so much noise I thought it would explode. *But wait, we are in an overloaded Huey, and this is the Army.* Pushing the limits is what you do!

As our choppers began to shutter and lift-off, our skilled aviators tilted the nose in a downward motion to pull maximum air across the rotor to gain elevation. It took an extraordinary amount of time and distance to get airborne. Fortunately, there was a cliff at the end of our short course, and the sudden drop off the edge enabled the choppers to gain speed and altitude before crashing.

In addition to avoiding the most intense enemy fire, our pilots did a superb job of avoiding the tree stumps and butterfly bombs that could have ended our flight. Once again, we survived another close call, and no one was injured. It was the best joy ride of my life. *Wow, I couldn't wait to do that again. NOT!*

Every member of the air-mobile infantry will confirm their love for the worthiness of the Huey helicopter and the guts of the guys that flew them. I am no exception. The (HU-1A) Huey used to transport troops and supplies was also called a "slick" due to its lack of the heavy armament of a Huey gunship.

From my perspective, the Huey was indestructible. I'm sure the pilots would've had a different analysis. Unless an RPG or a bullet hit the rotor gearbox, they could really take a pounding.

The Huey was a real workhorse. It brought relief supplies and chow, removed our wounded from the battlefield and transported us wherever we needed to go. Some were outfitted with rocket pods and mini-guns and were called gunships.

These air combat assault choppers saved our butts on many occasions—a lot of firepower in a small package. The Huey flew fast and low just above the trees, which made it difficult for enemy gunfire to hit them. I always loved flying in a Huey and still believe they are the safest combat mode of transportation around. The pilots, of course, were daring and capable. All appeared to be young and fearless, although I suspect, like us, they crapped their drawers on more than one occasion.

I can personally confirm that a Huey can take a licking and keep on ticking. I say this as I reflect upon another harrowing experience during an air assault insertion. As was customary, I was sitting on the floor of the Huey with my butt carefully located on my steel pot. My legs were stretched out in front of me. This was the usual protocol for young men who wish to protect their manhood and capacity to father children someday.

Suddenly, I could see several little holes appearing between my legs. The chopper started taking ground fire, and the bullets were coming through the floor, between my legs and up through the roof into the rotor blades. Severe damage to the blades put the chopper out of balance and caused a lot of vibration. Although severely damaged, the chopper kept flying, and we made it to the LZ. I specifically remember staring in amazement at the holes in the floor just inches from my legs and family jewels.

It was yet one more unforgettable moment that I quickly added it to my personal "way too close for comfort" list. I also remember how happy I was to jump out of that helicopter into the LZ.

Huey slicks getting ready to extract us from an LZ.

Chapter 12

FNGs and DEROS

Typically, and in the early days of assignment (1965) to Vietnam, the First Infantry Division and other combat divisions of the US military deployed to Vietnam as complete combat units. The rationale was to create a more cohesive fighting unit by having soldiers train and work together. In theory, they would then fight better together. I think this is true. In WWII and Korea, for example, soldiers stayed in the Army until the war was over or they became a casualty or fatality. Each soldier bonded with his unit companions. They shipped out together, and they came home together. The morale was good, and each member of the unit looked out for their pals. No matter the war, the underlying goal was to help each other survive and come home.

In Vietnam, however, the Army set a "time in combat date" at one year. At the end of one year, soldiers were rotated out of their unit, and someone new would take their place. This system provided certainty regarding an individual's length of tour in Vietnam. However, this approach did not foster the cohesiveness of a battle unit that trained and deployed as one team. A new replacement was greeted into the platoon as the "Fucking New Guy" (FNG). He was promptly assigned all the less desirable and sometimes more dangerous tasks, like burning shit or setting up a Listening Post (LP) outside the perimeter. Toting ammo for the machine gunner was another tough job assigned to the FNG, as was carrying extra mortar rounds or the base plate for the 81MM mortar tubes.

A little more description of burning shit is warranted. Specifically, the task was identified as burning solid waste from the latrines when back in base camp. The latrines were outfitted under each hole, with the bottom third of a barrel strategically positioned to catch the waste. Every other day, these waste storage receptacles were pulled from their duty position outside of the latrine and burned. Diesel fuel was the combustible fuel of choice. This was a necessary task and definitely a shitty job! The smell was awful and burning one's uniform was the first step in getting the smell off your body once the task was completed.

The FNG hazing did not usually apply to new medics. There were not that many of us, and our military job was so specialized. Maybe I was treated better than most FNGs because the other soldiers knew it was not productive to mess with a medic whose ability to exact revenge was obvious. I had the power to give my friendly foes the needle if you get the point.

I was sent to my line unit immediately because there was no overlap with the old company or platoon medic and the new one. The real challenge was to earn the respect of the men for whom I was medically responsible. The medic I replaced had done a fine job introducing me to the soldiers in my platoon. He had also explained the nuances of my job and some of the personal quirks of the men. Nobody, however, can explain the conditions of combat or how best to do your job as a medic under these conditions. Like most things in war, I would have to figure that out myself.

FNGs often became resentful of the orders and tasks to which they were assigned. These were fighting men and not disposers of human waste. This system of harassing the FNG did not foster goodwill. The ultimate saving grace occurred when a soldier moved from FNG to "brother-in-arms," which enabled that elevated soldier to harass his replacement FNG. Some historical Army customs are destined to repeat themselves.

Pulling point, flank guard, LP or ambush were the most dangerous assignments in the infantry. As such, the problem created with this "tour and rotation out" system was compounded by the fact that many of the best, most experienced soldiers were happy to let the FNG assume these jobs. Unfortunately, inexperience in such critical positions could put the entire patrol in even more danger. While you can't fault the "short-timers," on occasion, the lack of FNG experience exposed patrols to booby traps or led them into an ambush that a more seasoned soldier would have avoided.

Even though giving FNGs the more dangerous jobs is a time-honored military tradition, the approach is probably flawed because it substituted time in country for experience. But this is the Army and soldiers do what they are asked. We all knew you had to pay your dues for admission to the elite club of "combat veteran." We also knew you paid your dues by taking your turn in the barrel of danger. Nevertheless, the will to survive is strong among members of a fighting unit.

Since the one-year rotation was Army protocol, we all counted days until DEROS, which stood for the "Date Eligible for Return from Overseas." For most of us, the end date could not come soon enough. Your DEROS was uppermost in your mind, and every soldier knew exactly how many days they had left in country. I always felt screwed by the Army because my year in country was a leap year, which resulted in my anxiety lasting an extra day.

It was always a sad occurrence when a short-timer became a casualty or fatality. But that is war for you. You never knew when or how combat would turn a good day into a very bad day.

Chapter 13

The Danger of Snakes and Indigenous Reptiles

Snakes, I learned early, were a routine part of the hostile encounters I'd experience in Vietnam. I'm from Minnesota and grew up with lots of snakes as a kid—bull snakes, garter snakes and even an occasional red-belly snake. But none of these can harm a person, let alone kill him. There are no poisonous snakes in Minnesota except for an occasional rattlesnake in the river bluffs of the southeastern part of the state. Snake sightings are rare, and bites are rarer still.

In Vietnam, however, there are more than a hundred species of snakes, and more than forty of them are venomous. This makes navigating the jungle much more dangerous than hiking the prairies of Minnesota. Not only can Vietnamese snakes harm you, but they can also kill you. Unlike rattlesnakes, the snakes in Vietnam would strike without warning. In jungle survival school, I learned about several species of common serpents that were extremely deadly. "Don't mess with them" was our simple instruction. Medical training at Ft. Sam taught me how to handle a snakebite victim, and in Vietnam, I put that training to good use. While all of my snakebite patients survived, none of the slithering serpents escaped the wrath of the stricken soldier.

While on patrol one day, the lieutenant told us to take a break. Since we'd been humping the boonies for a few hours, I looked forward to gorging myself on some of fine C-rations, then have a smoke and hopefully a short nap. One of our riflemen decided to flop down on the ground without looking first. You guessed it—he landed on top of a colorful pit viper. You guessed it again—the snake struck him on the right cheek of his ass. After a gunshot, the snake was KIA.

At the sound of the shot, however, the entire patrol sprang into full alert prepared to do battle with the Viet Cong. In a combat zone, gunshots are a no-no unless you are returning fire at an enemy hostile. Once calm was restored, I was summoned to the site of the dead snake and a soldier in obvious distress.

The snakebite victim was in a fair amount of pain and a lot of panic. The bite mark, which looked like a rattlesnake, told me I knew it was from a pit viper. I needed to start treatment quickly, but death was not imminent. When I discovered the location of the bite, I had the GI drop his pants and sliced an X across the fang marks. Using a suction bulb, I drew poison and blood from the point of entry. The updated Army had provided helpful little tools like "suction bulbs" in our snake kit so we wouldn't have to use our mouths in the age-old practice of sucking and spitting. Both techniques were effective in removing much of the poison, thereby slowing its spread through the bloodstream.

My panicking casualty asked, "Are you going to play John Wayne and suck the poison out of the wound with your mouth like in the cowboy movies?"

I said, "Not a chance." If that was necessary, I'd get an FNG to do it.

After pulling out the poison, I applied a wound cleansing agent, applied a battle bandage and called for a dust-off for the concerned sufferer. As I expected, he survived and returned to the platoon about a week later, fully armed with his new war story about the *real* enemies of Vietnam! Although he did not get a Purple Heart for his injury, he was the recipient of lots of praise like, "Way to go, idiot!" The moral of this story: *Look before you sit!*

One of my most frightening snake encounters occurred just after digging our foxholes near a bridge on the Song Be River. One of my troopers asked to borrow my flashlight. No soldiers but the officers and platoon sergeants were trusted to carry a flashlight because when illuminated, the light could be seen by the enemy from quite a distance. I needed a flashlight to be able to treat a casualty at night. Even then, I used a red filter to diminish the brightness.

When I asked the FNG why he needed my flashlight, he said, "As I finished digging my foxhole, I noticed a snake in the bamboo thicket nearby, and I can't sleep knowing that thing is there."

"Sorry," I said, "you still can't have my flashlight. But I'll help you survey the area to see if I can spot it." My nervous cohort retrieved a shovel, and I grabbed a machete as my weapon of choice. We quietly set off to administer death to our hostile intruder. Since it was now totally dark, our mission was dangerous and required stealth and cunning. Not a problem, of course, because we were both well-trained in the art of ambush patrols. This adventure would be less dangerous, so we thought—after all, it was just a snake.

As we approached the bamboo thicket, I turned on my red-filtered flashlight and began a systematic search for the slithering critter. After spotting it, I told my teammate to place his shovel under the snake and then toss it into the clearing behind me so I could get a whack at him. The plan worked exceedingly well. The snake was easily removed from his lair and deposited in the clearing. So far, so good. By this time, though, it occurred to me that our plan was neither well-thought-out or rehearsed.

I had the flashlight in my left hand and my machete poised for action in my right hand. Imagine my amazement when the beam of my flashlight illuminated the snake already in the strike position. The light got the snake's attention, and a hood popped out around its head. I thought, *Holy crap! Is that a cobra ready to bite me?*

Fortunately, my reaction was quicker than the snake's. With one quick swipe of the machete, I cut off its head. Needless to say, I mentally recorded that incident in my book of life experiences and remember it vividly to this day.

After careful reflection about what just occurred, I concluded I had to develop a much safer "slithering search-and-destroy battle plan" if I was going to survive my tour. My new approach was "caution," and it was highly effective. I never had such a hazardous reptile encounter again. Once more, on-the-job training was the best teacher.

Another time, while on a night mission, we set up our ambush in an area that had been decimated by several Napalm bombs. The terrain was burned to a crisp, making it difficult to maintain silence. We finally got into position and formed our firing line, which extended about fifteen feet. The mosquitoes soon moved into position as well and inflicted numerous bites upon our combat-hardened group. The bugs were particularly bad that night, so we all kept our liquid repellant at the ready. That was a good idea because what happened next made for a very interesting evening.

As we lay prone in our night position, contemplating life and trying to stay vigilant, someone on the right side of our line whispered that they had movement in front of him. The guys in the middle said the same thing, and the grunts on the left soon reported the same observation. We could hear the gentle crunch of something crawling across the entire front of our patrol.

You don't want to shoot and give away your position unless you're committed to blowing the ambush and retreating to the perimeter. When you disclose your position, the enemy has the advantage. None of us, however, thought our intruder was an enemy soldier. It was more likely a snake. In the darkness, imaginations can go wild. So, what to do? We surely didn't want to just lie there and let some large constrictor coil around one of us and squeeze the life out.

I suggested we all take out our mosquito repellant and squirt it at the same time at the low-crawling enemy. As the platoon leader loudly whispered, "SQUIRT," we all emptied our newly christened battle weapons. A moment later, success! The snake quickly left the area with much louder crawling sounds. It must have been a large python, but our reptile repellant worked perfectly. That was the only action to occur that evening, and we were thankful. Always vigilant and now fearing new threats, none of us got much sleep that night.

Chapter 14

Turning 21: My Age of Enlightenment

On November 29, 1967, I turned twenty-one years old. With just four months under my Vietnam tour belt, I had quickly aged beyond my actual years. I was combat-hardened and excelled at camping in the wilderness. As a kid and teenager, I could hardly wait to reach my twenty-first birthday. It meant freedom, self-reliance and the ability to buy beer. Interestingly, in Vietnam, a person tends to lose track of important events like birthdays. Days run together, and it was difficult to tell Tuesday from Friday. But the calendar date was always memorable because it allowed us to continue the countdown toward completion of our tour of duty.

Imagine my surprise when I received my "birthday care package" from my mother on my actual birthday. I remember the occasion well. The package was another exceptional luxury that not only included the usual cookies, sardines and crackers, but also Slim Jim beef sticks, smoked oysters, a small bottle of vodka and a jar of Tang. Along with Mom's birthday greetings, she instructed me to mix a Screwdriver to celebrate my birthday.

I was practiced at following orders, so I mixed a big Tang and vodka cocktail and enjoyed its warming flavor—I didn't have any ice. I had never known Tang was such a multi-purpose beverage.

That fond expression of love from my mother was truly special. It disrupted the boredom that day by bringing a degree of normalcy from home.

The care package also contained a baseball signed by all the ladies on my mother's All-Star bowling team. It was nice to feel the love from so many people, especially in a place where love and expressions of kindness were lacking. It's wonderful to remember every detail of one of the good things that happened in a location so full of danger and hostility.

Chapter 15

The Battle of the Beasts

Sometime in September, we were assigned to secure a Vietnamese voting poll. Our orders were clear: "Protect the locals from Viet Cong harassment." Our platoon milled around in the village until the boredom was finally broken by gunfire from a sniper attempting to discourage the local population from voting. Guess you don't see that back home. But then again, I witnessed many incidents in Vietnam that I couldn't imagine taking place in Minnesota. Consistent with my now standard operating procedure, I went on full alert and moved to the sound of gunfire to see if anybody needed medical attention. I was relieved that nobody was hurt, and the hostile threat was eliminated.

Soon thereafter, I walked around the corner of a hooch and stopped dead in my tracks ten feet from a water buffalo. I'm sure he weighed fifteen hundred pounds and had a seven-foot rack of horns. There was a mama san nearby with a stick in her hand. She was obviously working that animal to till a small garden plot adjacent to her abode.

As I stood in fear and awe, the beast—agitated by my presence—pawed at the dirt with gigantic front hooves while snorting and blowing snot all over. But I'm a Minnesota boy who had been on many farms. I knew how cows and bulls acted when threatened, so I was always careful about avoiding these threats, even though some bulls cast a wary eye. However, this time I knew a direct confrontation was unavoidable. The first rule in such a pending disaster is to petition that all-protecting "higher power" for mercy during your time of need. The second rule was, "Get the hell out of there!" Rule one was easy to implement. Rule two, not so much. I was paralyzed as I realized there was no time for a full-scale retreat. Even though my life didn't flash before my eyes, I believed I had only seconds before I would become the victim of this animal's irritation.

Not willing to go down without a fight, I pulled out my trusty but not sufficiently powerful .45 caliber pistol. As I raised it to dispatch the water buffalo, the mama san jumped between me and the beast. I didn't speak Vietnamese, but I could tell she didn't want me to shoot her dependable agricultural asset. Medics are pretty smart guys and Army-trained to react in perilous situations. As my brain began to function again, I put the pistol back in my holster. The mama san turned around to square off with the water buffalo. She smacked it hard on the nose, and to my amazement, the critter calmed down and backed away. That was something to behold.

Later, I discovered the importance of water buffalo to Vietnamese farmers and was told they have a gentle disposition. That might be true, but the eighty-five pound, four-and-a-half-foot mama san was one of the bravest persons I met in country. It was but one more interesting experience to file in my book of war memories.

In early February, right after the TET offensive that started on January 30, 1968, we were sent to an area called the Iron Triangle. Tet is a holiday to celebrate the Vietnamese New Year. Our orders for this search-and-destroy mission included securing the Michelin Rubber Plantation and blocking the path of any remnant NVA forces trying to retreat from the Saigon area. One morning after patrolling through some jungle brush, we entered the plantation where they harvested rubber from trees. This plantation was owned and operated by former French colonialists. It was an amazing place with acres of rubber trees planted in perfect ordered rows so each tree could get maximum sun and water.

The underbrush was virtually non-existent because of the abundance of shade. This layout also provided adequate space for equipment and personnel to move around and harvest the rubber. Once all of us were safely in the plantation, the platoon lieutenant told us to take a five-minute break. I squatted next to a tree and focused on the rubber slowly flowing along a carefully cut spiral groove in the tree bark that ended in a collection bowl about three feet off the ground. I lit a cigarette and began to enjoy the serenity of the place.

Suddenly, I heard a loud rustling noise to my rear. I feared an enemy bayonet charge and steeled myself for the onslaught. It was happening so fast that I didn't have time to shoot or throw a grenade. The noise grew louder. I knew the assassin was close, and I was in a real pickle.

Simultaneously, I watched a lieutenant who had heard the noise swing his AR-15 assault rifle toward my position. His eyes were as big as saucers.

Finally, I dove to the other side of the rubber tree to protect myself. The lieutenant shot several rounds, and the intruder ran to the left flank where he was met with a hail of automatic gunfire and.

Thanks to my quick reaction and the sharp-shooting of my brothers, that one hundred fifty-pound wild boar and with eight-inch fangs failed to injure me.

After I cleaned my soiled pants, a couple of us retrieved the freshly shot antagonist and presented him to the locals. The boar fed several villages. I now fully understood why they called every place outside Saigon a "hostile environment."

Chapter 16

More Unseen Dangers and Hidden Treasures

Going on a patrol requires every soldier to be vigilant and tap into his natural sense of sight, smell and sound. Any movement or sound can be a threat that can TAKE YOU OUT. On patrol, soldiers also rely on their combat brothers to warn the rest of the patrol to any danger and react quickly to hazards.

The most immediate danger, of course, is walking into an ambush, encountering a sniper, or stepping on a mine or booby-trap. The routine order of the day was, "Eliminate any threat, evacuate the wounded, and the patrol continues its mission." Sometimes the threats we faced required more analysis before response. The perils we faced were much different from the perils we would have faced back home in the States. We all needed to adjust to this different kind of threat by exercising more caution and using more brainpower.

Two examples of these threats were tripwires attached to bombs or grenades, and punji sticks buried in a pit. I learned about these hazards in jungle school, but the danger they posed didn't strike home until I encountered them in the bush. You had to develop a gut instinct for identifying these hidden dangers or, more likely, rely on Lady Luck.

We were constantly exposed to homemade antipersonnel or booby trap devices. Sadly, the misfortunes of other soldiers seemed to be the best teacher. The VC were very experienced in jungle warfare. They knew how best to use a small explosive charge to inflict damage on the unsuspecting. Most of the time, these devices caused nuisance injuries and were intended to slow down the patrol. All too often, the observant enemy would then greet us with bigger and better deadly surprises down the trail.

One time, our point man came across a tripwire. He knew that it led to a bomb that would kill anyone who tripped the wire. The point man's job was to mark the location and pass the word to the next man so he could avoid the booby trap. Each soldier, in turn, showed the next grunt where the tripwire was and pointed out which way to go.

I remember slowly stepping over the wire so the 105-mm howitzer round it was attached to would not explode. It was a crude device but highly effective at killing unwary soldiers. The enemy was shrewd and frequently used one of our American-made artillery rounds to bomb our patrol. The undetonated bomb was suspended about a foot off the ground from a tree branch adjacent to a trail. The fins of the bomb pointed upward and nose downward. The nose cone contained the detonator that would explode when the bomb impacted a solid surface. This particular kind of booby trap was set up to allow the bomb to fall about three feet to the ground once someone disturbed the tripwire that would, in turn, pull out the pin that was holding the bomb in place. Primitive but clever. In this particular instance, our capable point man saw the tripwire and recognized the booby trap. Once again, his uncanny ability to recognize danger prevented injury or death.

During my time in the bush, we encountered many such devices, but keen eyes from the point men generally prevented misfortune. It was too bad for the VC because our practice was to re-set the device in a different spot so an unsuspecting hostile patrol would fall prey to their own booby traps. I don't know if that ever happened, but the boys always felt better about it.

On another occasion, my platoon was on a search-and-destroy mission near the Cambodian border in the "Hill Country." We were told that morning to be on the lookout for Montagnards—indigenous people living in the area. These people were intensely loyal to Americans and fierce enemies of the North Vietnamese who had been attacking them for centuries. Montagnards served as guides for Army of the Republic of Vietnam (ARVN) forces and American combat units.

On patrol, nothing seemed out of the ordinary, but we all had that uneasy feeling of being watched. Being on edge was a good thing in such times. Our point man parted some bushes and got the crap scared out of him when he came face to face with three Montagnard hunters. Surprisingly, no gunfire was accidentally exchanged, and curiosity took over.

These stealthy men were slight in stature, standing about four-feet-six and weighing a whopping ninety pounds, I think. They did not carry guns, just primitive weapons—a spear, a crossbow and a blow gun. Those weapons looked scarier to us than an AK-47 in a VC's hands.

These fellows were older men who protected their area and hunted for food while the younger Montagnards served as guides for US combat units. They didn't speak English, and we didn't speak their unique brand of Vietnamese. I did note a hint of French in their dialect, but true to form, no one in my unit spoke French either.

We could, however, communicate basic messages and understood their desire to have us follow them. Their village was a hundred yards down the trail—more of a hamlet designed for security and family community. The space was carved out of the jungle and consisted of six elevated structures on stilts. These simple living units were constructed with bamboo and thatched roofs. But to the inhabitants, I'm sure, they were as elegant as any housing we enjoyed back home. They were clean and functional, complete with cooking, sleeping and dining spaces. Several small gardens containing vegetables were scattered amongst the huts, each competing for sunlight. This pristine, peaceful place was miles from other towns or villages. I was honored to bear witness to how they lived.

I felt like I was researching an article for *National Geographic* about the shy, indigenous people of the Vietnam highlands. The men wore loincloths, and so did the women. All were lean and tough. They did not have any foot protection, and the women were bare-breasted. One young mother was nursing a baby. I was very touched by these people and amazed by their tranquil disposition and the serenity of their village in the middle of a deadly war. Maybe it was easy to maintain this zest for life if you can stay hidden in the jungle and take advantage of the resources you could harvest.

We followed our newly found bush guides to the center of the village where we met the elder. He was the man in charge, so to speak, and his friendly disposition helped us relax. When our lieutenant asked about the VC, the elder pointed to let us know they were in the area. I seldom carried my camera on patrol, but on this day, it was with me. I snapped a few pictures of the people and their huts, which have allowed me to revisit this memory many times.

We continued our mission, heading in the direction of the VC pointed out by the elder. We were later told that we may have been the first Americans the Montagnard had ever encountered. For sure, it was the only time we ever encountered these unique bush people. What a great experience.

Chapter 17

Breaking My Combat Cherry

I think every person in the military has wondered how he or she would act under fire. With my vivid imagination, lots of things went through my mind. Knowing I was in an infantry company in Vietnam guaranteed that I would experience combat sooner or later.

The seasoned Blue Spader combat veterans in Company A talked about their experiences and rehashed what it was like, how they survived, and the damage they had inflicted on the enemy. Each firefight had provided a new learning experience that increased their chances of surviving.

Hearing their reflections made me more fearful. I hoped that I wouldn't be a coward, unable to discharge my duties. Fear and paranoia were personal things, and I was just as fearful and paranoid as the next guy. I often wondered, *What is combat really like?* Lacking in the actual experience, one's mind easily conjures images about these kinds of life and death matters. Soon, one becomes the main actor in this rare drama. The soldier trains for battle but can only guess how he will act. Waiting and anticipating this unknown becomes foremost in one's mind, and the anxiety can consume you.

Would you stand and fight? Would you leap into action and administer aid to a wounded buddy? Or would fear overwhelm you and handicap your actions?

Suddenly, you are cast into battle and get the answers to these questions. No more speculation; newly found certainty and purpose.

When my big day arrived, I realized that nothing had adequately prepared me for how to cope with that first burst of enemy gunfire. The deafening noise under hostile circumstances seemed like controlled chaos. I can't fully explain it but breaking my "combat cherry" was nothing like what I had imagined.

My first combat experience was incredible. We were ambushed by a couple of enemy snipers that had plenty of time to plan while we had almost no time to react. But that was the way firefights usually unfolded. My clothes got so drenched in sweat, I looked like I had just swum in a river. My hands shook, and my heart pounded so hard I thought it would burst from my chest and run back to base camp. My eyes were as big as softballs, and I believed every gunshot was a threat personally directed at me. It was chaos, for sure, but for some crazy reason, our response seemed organized at the same time. The adrenaline rush really charged me up and nearly made me feel invincible.

In combat, though, you quickly learn a little adrenaline is a good thing but only in moderation. Too much survival juice and you become paralyzed and unable to act intelligently or think clearly. Even worse, you do stupid things. No training can prepare you for the experience of this chemically enhanced courage. People who've been exposed to a "life-threatening" incident probably know the feeling. Quickly, you realize you are not dead or wounded. Your body vital signs start to normalize. You survive the battle and, most importantly, over time, you learn how to manage the anxiety and fear. By necessity, you learn to let your training kick in. Not an easy task.

My first firefight was the most traumatic, but future ones didn't get easier—I just developed better coping skills. In this first battle, confusion, fear and uncertainty hit me full square. I heard the initial burst of fire and became keenly aware of the smell of gunpowder.

Surviving the initial burst was the key. Most of the causalities occurred in the first few moments of the firefight.

Even as a medic, I eventually was able to discern harassing fire and an all-out attack. It only took a few weeks to become exposed to the intensity and scale of combat. When you are in the infantry, you are eventually going to gain this experience. Remember, the Army strongly believes in the principal of "on-the-job training." With the Big Red One, you were on the job all the time.

As gunshots seemingly came from every direction, I dove to the ground faster and harder than a hawk can hit a rabbit. Instinct and training took charge, and I checked to make sure I didn't get hit. All body parts seemed to be in working order.

It didn't take long for me to realize the ground was my friend. Once a soldier is in a prone position on the ground, it becomes very difficult for bullets to find him. That's a good thing, but he's not out of harm's way yet. He soon discovers that enemy grenades and mortars remain a threat.

Obviously, I survived my initial encounter with a hostile force. The experience, however, helped me understand that war was a very personal affair. It was kill or be killed. While skill helped immensely, luck played an even more significant role in surviving a firefight.

Regrettably, my first combat experience required me to operate as a "hopeful lifesaver." Shortly after the initial burst of enemy gunfire, I heard my first scream for a medic. Gunfire and screams for the medic were new experiences for me.

Without thinking, I abandoned my safe haven behind some trees and rushed to an injured soldier. In this case, my first wounded combatant was lucky because he had sustained relatively minor gunshot wounds to his leg and arm, neither of which was life-threatening. He had no broken bones, was breathing on his own and verbally shouted profanities at the Viet Cong. I agreed with his insults, so I guess that was a good thing. The arm injury was just a graze and, the leg injury exposed several inches of muscle. I had never seen torn tissue before.

I was able to control the bleeding by applying pressure and tightly securing the field dressings with an ACE bandage. Next to morphine, these stretch wraps were the ultimate utility tool for a medic. There was no need to start an IV because the soldier had not lost much blood. He was not in shock and not in much pain, so I kept my morphine pack in my pocket.

Following protocol, I asked the platoon radio operator (PRO) to call for a dust-off. This was another new experience for me. The air extraction procedure was simple and routine. I was handed the mic so I could talk to the pilots and instruct them to land at the site of a purple smoke grenade that marked my location.

A "Huey dustoff" is circling and ready to pick up a casualty.

Once I got my "patient" on the chopper, my job was done for a moment. I could catch my breath. Plopped onto the ground, I drank all the water from one of my four canteens, lit a cigarette and then tried to calm down and reflect on what the hell had just happened.

Thoughts raced through my mind. *I think I just passed my first combat test, and I didn't pass out at the sight of blood. What an experience! I guess I'll tuck that away in my mind, so I can relive it some time again fifty years from now. I wonder what my buddies are doing back home this afternoon. Bet whatever it was, their day wasn't nearly as exciting mine.*

I knew it was going to be a very long year if this shit kept happening. In my unit, I was still considered a "long-timer" because I was only a couple of weeks in country. But I felt like I still had a million days to go before my tour was up and I could go home.

The battle was over as quickly as it started, which was frequently the case. I had experienced combat, and I had treated and evacuated my first casualty. It was early September, and I had only been with my unit for a couple of weeks. But I had lost my cherry and discovered my answer to the perplexing question about how I would respond the first time I was in combat. I did not panic and, more importantly, I did my job. I didn't yet understand the importance of my actions on the rest of the unit. I was no longer just an FNG; I was now my brothers' hope for survival. I had established myself as a combat medic and demonstrated to the platoon that they could count on me. I felt relieved and privileged at the same time.

As the days and weeks passed, I gained more knowledge and confidence. The soldiers of Company A, Lima Platoon, now realized this medic had their back. A special bond usually develops between soldiers and the medic. For the riflemen, having a medic on patrol is a physical and psychological necessity. For me, it was strenuous and distressing.

Did I really volunteer to be a medic? Where is my hospital duty?

After my first battle, all future firefights were just repeated moments of sheer terror accompanied by lots of noise and chaos. But I understood now that I had joined a very elite club. I had earned my combat medical badge. Infantrymen who had experienced combat received the "Combat Infantry Badge" bearing a rifle and a wreath. Medics received a "Combat Medical Badge" bearing a Medical

Caduceus symbol and a stretcher. I never would have obtained this special recognition had I served in a hospital in Italy or Germany. I still cherish my CMB. It is the military recognition of which I am most proud.

The ultimate experience of that first firefight was tough but important. Guess I was now ready for grad school!

With more combat experience, I was amazed at how calm I could be in a crisis. During these episodes, every soldier quickly discovers prayer and hopes for a good outcome. Curiously, in every firefight, I prayed to God, Buddha, Allah, the Sun, the Stars, the Trees and the Rocks. I was not leaving anything or any possible deity to chance. I was confident in my belief that one of these gods would be the true Supreme Being who controlled my fate. It's best, though, not to become a causality in the first place!

Combat also taught me to admire American firepower and the willingness to apply it in great quantities when called upon. Airplanes, gunships and artillery all brought comfort when applied to the battle at hand. These instruments of destruction usually brought an end to the firefight. Whenever I felt the heat of a Napalm bomb hitting close to my position, I knew there was nothing between me and that explosion. N-a-p-a-l-m is how I spelled relief!

I would like to point out that only in a war zone can a twenty-two-year-old second lieutenant spend a million dollars on a sniper!

Chapter 18

On-the-Job Training

Combat required me to grow up fast and to do things I never imagined I could do. No medical training or life experience really prepares you for the things you encounter in a world of trauma and hurt. While I might have been scared to death, I knew I had to act quickly and intelligently, always understanding that failure was not an option. I couldn't phone a friend, and every decision was hard. I couldn't call for help because I was the help everyone called on.

My "on-the-job training" accelerated my education. Those experiences taught me the importance of making decisions and finishing the task at hand. Mistakes? I made a few, but I also learned to live with the consequences. Looking back at my life, I must credit those valuable tutorials as the reason I have never encountered a problem I couldn't handle. Guess that's one benefit of war.

I often thought the ten weeks of combat medical training was insufficient. But then again, the Army is very good at providing opportunities for soldiers to continue honing their professional skills through on-the-job training. So often, the tasks at hand in Vietnam required me to do more than I ever thought I could do. Typically, it was just me. BOOM, loud noise, hit the deck, machine gun fire… I'm not hit, catch a breath. Listen for the call for "medic," look around and begin working. It is a very lonely feeling when you realize medical

back-up (like a real doctor or a hospital) might be hours away. STOP
THE BLEEDING. *Yes, but how?* My battle dressings seem so deficient.
PAIN. *How do I manage the pain?* Morphine. Ah yes, morphine. Give
mouth to mouth. Handle it… get him on the medivac helicopter and
pray that he makes it.

I knew if my casualty was alive when I got him on the dust-off, he
had a 92 percent chance of surviving. Only then could I let my guard
down and relax. I needed to let my body recover from the adrenaline
explosion, the stress of the event, the madness of it all. Now, let God
and the others take care of him. My part is over.

But not all combat encounters were in the bush. One time at
our base camp, a guy went psycho and threatened to shoot anyone
who tried to send him back into combat. Since he was a soldier in
our battalion, he was considered one of "my guys." As such, the MPs
instructed me to go into his tent where he was waving a pistol around
and talk him into putting it back in its holster.

I told the MPs, "You go into his hooch, grab him and I'll
administer a shot of Thorazine to calm him down."

The MPs rationalized it would be too dangerous for them to grab
him because he'd most likely open fire on them.

I thought, *Well, isn't that what MPs do? Weren't they trained to
confront danger? Wasn't their job to secure the threat?*

NO. The chicken shits were thinking that the distraught soldier
probably wouldn't harm me because I was a medic, and medics are
trustworthy and important to every soldier. Besides, by this time in
my tour, I was known as a man of persuasive words. *Let's just let Doc
apply his skills to this situation.*

With that compliment, how could I refuse to lead the way for the
hesitant military police officers and talk the distraught soldier to put
his pistol away?

The MPs and I finally achieved consensus on a plan. The
implementation, though, was a little scary, to say the least. I went into
the hooch first and approached the armed soldier. He was waving the

pistol and shouting that he had to "get out of this place!" Apparently, he didn't care how, and the truth is, we all wanted to get out of "this place."

To this day, I wonder if he was crazy or if the rest of us were. Even though he was obviously upset, he never pointed the gun at me. If he had, I am not sure what I would have done.

As I approached him, I continued to talk in a calm voice. I remember telling him, "We all feel the stress, my friend, but most of us choose other methods to deal with it."

Some guys I knew chose hookers and booze. Others chose the church and the Bible—not nearly as often. But hey, who am I to judge?

When I got right next to the troubled soldier, I asked him to give me the pistol. To my surprise and relief, he did. As I took the .45 out of his hand, the MPs stormed through the door like the brave lads they were and tackled him. I too piled on this trembling soldier now spread out on the floor and grabbed a leg. Since there were now eight legs in the pile, I had to make sure the leg I grabbed was HIS.

I injected a shot of Thorazine, which is good for mellowing out some not-so-mellow folks. I didn't use alcohol swabs or follow clinic protocol—I just stuck the needle through his pants and into his leg muscle. I pushed the plunger, and soon he was in "la la land." He immediately calmed down, and I sent him off to the hospital for further evaluation and treatment.

More "on-the-job training."

As a medic, you learn to follow your gut and hope for the best. The MPs bought me a bottle of Old Crow whiskey for that job. That's how we coped. Thankfully, none of us got shot. But by then, we were all used to living with danger.

As for the distressed soldier, I never saw him again.

Chapter 19

Gaining Perspective

Over the years, I have been asked by family, friends and strangers how I have coped with the insanity of combat. Did I ever feel helpless? The answer is an emphatic *yes*. I relive those memories every day and sometimes at night. But there is nothing I can do about it.

Whenever my unit made contact with the enemy on a search-and-destroy mission, all hell broke loose. As the battle gained intensity, we were all counting on each other to do our jobs. As the riflemen suppressed enemy fire, medics jumped into action. I felt the enormous weight of my job every time a man went down. There were no second chances, but plenty of everlasting memories of "should haves" or "could haves." Nevertheless, I accepted my obligation and resolved to treat every injury as best I could, even if I was winging it.

Placing IVs during a firefight was nearly impossible, and just about every attempt was unsuccessful. Often, as I was trying to insert a needle, we were still receiving fire. After the war, I reflected on my frustrating inability to start battlefield IVs and concluded that my casualty was in shock or my adrenaline was pumping so hard I was nearly in shock myself. *I guess that is why they call it combat triage.* I learned to fully accept the challenge and simply do what I could. I learned not to overthink the situation. After all, I always had morphine to ease their pain.

Because we were part of the Big Red One, we were destined to be in combat. Search-and-destroy was a daily option. Firefights pushed all of us to the limits. We needed to think clearly and then constructively react. Sometimes it took every last ounce of mental and physical energy to complete my job and to survive the ordeal. There was tremendous added pressure in trying to save a man's life when saving it was next to impossible. For me, there was no turning back, and frequently, no time to think. I was at the beginning of the casualty chain with nobody to call on for advice.

"You are the medic, so deal with it!" Treat and evacuate.

Sometimes, my treatment magic worked, and I saved a life. Unfortunately, sometimes nothing I did could keep my brother out of the hands of God. I eventually learned to suck it up and move on. After all, I would have the rest of my life to analyze those situations and cope with the memories. But this meant bottling up that sense of frequent failure, shutting down all second-guessing and repressing all the lingering desperation and sadness. I think most combat veterans, medics and non-medics alike, feel the same way.

Chapter 20

The First Was the Worst

The following incidents provide some personal insight into the hardships of my job as a medic in combat and the continuous battle afterward to battle the surviving emotions that replay forever. Unfortunately, I can't change the reality of these stories, so the outcome is always the same.

During my one-year tenure in Vietnam, eighteen soldiers in my company were killed in action. I did not treat all of them because there were four medics in each company. From a combat perspective, that was a lot of good men who died in one year. I don't recall the total number of wounded, but there were many. The injuries varied in severity and type—from burns and lacerations to puncture wounds, abrasions, sucking chest wounds and severe head injuries. I treated many men I knew, and some I did not. Out of respect for the privacy of all these Purple Heart recipients, I have chosen not to identify them by name. But I do remember the despair we all felt on numerous occasions.

In every instance of combat, I tried my best to maintain a positive attitude. I always had hope and faith that my actions would result in a good outcome, but I admit to using prayer as my main backup. Not only did I have to control my own fear of the battle, but I also had to deal with the burden of fear that accompanied my recently wounded trustee. I recognized my vulnerability and worried about getting shot and killed myself. Interestingly, such thoughts were more prevalent at night in the relative safety of our Night Defensive Position (NDP). When a battle started, I never thought about such things, even though the possibility of getting hurt was obvious.

It didn't take me long to get combat and treatment smart. Just knowing what to expect in a firefight made difficult tasks manageable. As for attitude, I will forever feel honored to have had the privilege to help these soldiers in their time of need. It produced an intimate bond at a very personal once-in-a-lifetime moment. It wasn't just my job—it was a sacred duty.

Like most infantry companies in a war zone, Company A was woefully understrength. As I look back, I wonder how any of us made it home. You merely need to reflect on the politics of the war and the ego of a couple of our presidents to understand why we were put in that hellhole, to begin with. Combat was nasty, and the consequences could be devastating.

I will never forget the first soldier to die under my care. I vividly remember the ferociousness of the battle. I was with him when he was injured but not when he died. Maybe that made the situation even more frustrating. At the time, I couldn't understand the full measure of what it meant to be combat wounded because it happened so fast. But I learned to make the necessary adjustments and move on. Maybe it will make sense someday.

Our mission that night was to establish an ambush position. As the sun was setting, we still had not arrived at our predesignated ambush site. The danger had increased because the enemy could easily see us moving through their turf, but it was almost impossible for us to see them in the long shadows.

Experience told all of us this was not a good situation, and it was made more hazardous because our FNG platoon leader was a very gung-ho guy who desperately wanted to make contact with the enemy. As a result, three-quarters of the way to our ambush site, he made the decision to move deeper into enemy territory, hoping to engage hostiles. The situation report, and the intelligence he was furnished by battalion command, indicated there was a large concentration of Viet Cong operating in the area.

Although it was getting dark, this took us in a new direction, and, sure enough, we ended up at the wrong coordinates. Being out of position means your artillery and gunship support no longer knew your precise location, which made it very difficult to provide fire support in a timely manner. Eventually, it would arrive but would take more time, and time was very precious in combat.

We were in a free-fire zone, which meant we could fire at will and did not have to wait to be fired upon. Intel told us we were in a "hot area" and to be on full alert as if we weren't anyway. We were always on full alert! Sadly, a few months later, this gung-ho second lieutenant was killed by an uncaring and battle-hardened enemy. He took needless chances, which may have made him popular with commanders but distressingly unpopular among his platoon members. Even so, war and combat are not about popularity. War is about survival and body count.

Our squad of ten soldiers was moving quickly because we were sitting ducks. We crossed a road and entered an open field heading toward a woodline that could serve as cover for our night ambush. This cover was a mere two hundred meters away. We all knew we were vulnerable while crossing that field.

The situation was bad, and then it got worse. About a hundred yards to our left was a village surrounded by a berm from which the enemy could initiate an attack. We moved with caution, keeping our weapons on the village and potential disaster. As we began to cross, the rifleman next to me spotted a VC hostile pointing a machine gun at us.

He shouted, "Hit the dirt, Doc!"

We both safely plunged to the ground just as the enemy machine gun sent a killing burst our way. Bullets were flying everywhere. Since we were the target, the war had become intensely personal. Hot bullets and fragments were striking the dirt in front of us and ricocheting over our heads. The strikes were so close they threw dirt in my face.

Unfortunately, one of the bullets found their mark and hit the rifleman who had alerted us to the hostiles. He was shrieking in pain—I'll always remember his bloodcurdling screams—and tried to stand up, which would have made him an easier target. I reached up and pulled him back down.

I had to literally lay on top of him to hold him down and cut away his shirt to expose the wound and stop the bleeding. I finally got his shirt off and noticed a small entrance hole on the top left side of his shoulder between his neck and arm. But where the hell was the exit wound?

I was stymied for a few minutes. Dealing with gunshot wounds was another new experience for me. He was in so much pain I gave him morphine. The effects were immediate, and he to calmed down. But the damage was done. The bullet had not exited his body but instead rattled around inside, severely injuring tissue and vital organs.

Our squad formed a line of defense as another soldier helped me carry our wounded brother to a safer place behind the squad. I remember feeling intense fear as bullets kept flying around. Fortunately, the savagery of our return fire and counterattack affected the enemy's accuracy. I'm sure the VC had casualties too and kept their heads down or retreated, their more common practice. Despite the viciousness of the firefight, no one else was hit, thank God.

I knew my guy was bleeding internally, and we had to get him to a hospital as quickly as possible. Regrettably, during a firefight, "quickly as possible" is a relative term. I hated that part.

The first course of action was to suppress enemy fire, otherwise, it was too dangerous to bring in a dust-off helicopter to evacuate the rifleman. Medevac pilots were very skilled and brave, but they weren't stupid. I called for a dust-off, but the "all clear to land signal" took a while. This was my first experience dealing with such a catastrophic injury. I knew time was critical. The stress caused time to slow down—seconds seemed like minutes and minutes like hours. I felt helpless because I couldn't determine the full extent of his injuries.

Eventually, our coordinates were reestablished, and our lieutenant called in firepower to eliminate the threat. It took about forty minutes for our patrol, along with artillery and gunship support, to overwhelm the enemy. Finally, incoming fire stopped, and our insecure position along that road became quiet. I was finally able to call in a dust-off and get my severely injured soldier to a field hospital.

Because it was getting very dark, I was tasked with my first night medivac extraction. I was on the radio with the pilot describing my casualty's injuries and guiding the chopper in. Because the pilot needed to see the ground to land, he turned on his one million candlepower spotlight during the final fifty feet. This was flight protocol for the chopper but very unsettling for me as I became awash in light—a great target for the enemy. There was so much dust and noise I never would have heard an incoming bullet or RPG.

The field where we were ambushed became the place where we spent the night. Darkness provided concealment, but we had no other cover for protection. We had terminated the threat, but the village had been annihilated in the process.

I was encouraged because the rifleman who saved my life was still alive when we got him onto the dust-off chopper. More than an hour had passed since he'd been shot, and I knew he was going into shock. That brave soldier died later that night sometime after he reached the hospital. When I got the news of his death the following day, I felt like I'd been hit in the gut by a sledgehammer. I felt like shit. *He was still alive when I got him on the chopper, right? Better than a 92 percent chance of survival.* But statistics are only measurements of probability. That night, my combat charge was part of the 8 percent who would return to the "real world" in a pine box. War is mostly bullets and pine boxes.

I became very upset about losing my lifesaver. During the next few sleepless nights, new questions haunted me. *Did I do everything right? Could I have done more?* I felt like a failure, not up to the job. I became depressed over his death and did a lot of soul searching. After all, I'd been drafted and never asked to be put in this position.

After a few more days, a twenty-year medical sergeant sat me down and calmly shared his thoughts about dealing with my feelings. He knew how deeply this KIA had personally affected me and said I needed to understand a couple of combat facts.

"You are in a war," he said bluntly. "The soldier who died was not your brother, you did not shoot him, and most importantly, you did your best to save him under some pretty shitty circumstances. Now pull it together, or you won't be worth a damn to all of those other soldiers who are counting on you!"

That conversation was one of the hardest and most memorable conversations I ever had. It gave me a new perspective that would help me stay focused and keep moving forward.

During the remaining eleven months of my tour, I treated many more casualties and fatal injuries. I had no choice but to give it my all and deal with every new situation I encountered. Those incidents gave me a unique perspective on how to deal with the many challenges I faced in the years since coming home.

I can truthfully say that I learned how to deal with adversity in Vietnam. I always had to find some workable solution. I guess that's a good thing. *A silver lining?* Perhaps. One thing is certain—I think about those hard lessons every day.

Chapter 21

Mine Trouble

There were a couple different types of mines used in Vietnam. According to Captain Mike Fox in a paper he prepared for the Department of the Army in 1968, "The M-14 mine is a small, plastic mine containing two ounces of plastic explosive. This mine is not designed to kill a person, but it is highly effective as a disabling and demoralizing weapon. Approximately two inches in diameter and two inches thick, it is easily placed in the ground and armed, therefore making it a good weapon to employ in front of moving troops. Detection of the mine often depends upon the terrain. If the mine was recently put in place, small patches of disrupted grass or mounds of dirt may be found where it is buried. In Vietnam, this mine was not easily detected by a metallic mine detector."

The other type of mine was the M-16, also known as the "Bouncing Betty." It is a large, anti-personnel mine that weighs eight pounds, looks like a tomato can and is a highly effective weapon. It's armed with a pressure fuse detonator. When the fuse is activated by a soldier stepping on it, the main part of the mine is propelled approximately three feet into the air, where it explodes, covering the target area with fragmentation. These types of mines were downright deadly and led to many traumatic amputations of legs and arms. Fortunately, as foot soldiers, we seldom encountered any of these weapons, but all the mechanized units of the First Infantry Division did.

I do remember an incident that occurred when a group of M-113 armored personnel carriers (APCs) were speeding down Highway 13, a main artery in central Vietnam. The APCs, accompanied by a couple of tanks, were patrolling the road and moving between villages along the route. Intel had told us that the area was ripe with local VC and a full regiment of NVA.

On this bright, sunny day, my platoon was patrolling in the woodline about a hundred yards adjacent to the road. It's important to note that an armored troop carrier weighs about twelve tons, so it can easily detonate a land mine in its path. When VC are in the vicinity, APCs are like magnets for enemy fire, including rockets and mortars.

On this day, however, there were no VC present—only remnants of their nasty deeds were buried in the dirt. I remember watching the column of APCs move along the road and thinking, *Wow, that's a lot of firepower, but then again, they seem to always get a lot of attention from the enemy.*

Suddenly, one of the twelve-ton beasts hit a mine. The explosions were ear-piercing and unforgettable, the concussion enormous. My heart leaped into my throat, and other stuff went to my pants! Fortunately, on this day, only a track was injured, not soldiers. I still find it amazing that such a horrendous explosion can occur and injure no one, while at other times, one bullet can end the life of one of our finest.

Sometime in early October 1967, I treated a soldier who had stepped on an M-14 land mine while on patrol near Phouc Vinh. It happened in the middle of the day when the weather was clear. The patrol's objective was to cross a large, open area that consisted of rice paddies. The shortest route for the patrol was to cross a berm that ran between two rice paddies.

As the group approached the berm, the point man detonated a mine. Everyone hit the deck and readied themselves for combat. The riflemen pointed their rifles outward, clicked off their safeties and positioned hand grenades in front of them. On this day, no incoming fire was received. The only casualty was the soldier who had stepped on the mine.

Fortunately, (or perhaps unfortunately) the mine was an M-14. Some soldiers referred to these weapons as "toe-busters." Treating this kind of injury was another new experience for me. Soon after realizing the cause of the explosion, everyone froze in place and waited for an engineering team to clear the area.

I began to examine my new patient. The injured soldier was justifiably upset about what had just happened and concerned about the extent of his injury. Would he lose his foot?

I began to render aid and talked to him calmly and confidently to reduce his mild hysteria. I told him he would be OK—he shouldn't worry about dying. I explained how lucky he was because he had suffered a "million-dollar wound" that would send him stateside, never to return to combat.

As I began to treat his injury, I remember being genuinely amazed that the explosion had not amputated his foot. The boot technology really did work! Our GI jungle boots were fairly light and had a mesh side so moisture could weep out of the boot. This technology worked great during the monsoon season when we were constantly trudging through water and mud. The jungle boots occasionally gave our feet time to dry out, thereby avoiding open sores and trench foot.

More importantly, the boot had a flexible steel plate covering the entire bottom of the sole, which was designed to provide some protection from punji sticks or, as in this case, a small explosion. The injured soldier was not in a lot of pain, and the boot's design clearly had saved his foot. Rather than cut off the boot to more fully examine his injuries in the muck, it made more sense to simply wrap an Ace bandage around his boot to tightly hold his lacerated foot together. This stopped the bleeding, and I called for a dust-off.

I never learned what happened to this soldier. For the most part, the Army never told me what happened to any casualty I treated once they were evacuated from the battlefield. Maybe the Army thought such knowledge would psych me out. My opinion was that I could learn from the after-treatment care, which would increase my combat injury repertoire. But, like all things Army, "if the higher-ups thought it was a good idea to tell me about the outcome of those I treated, they would have done so." You just suck it up and move on.

Chapter 22

The First Battle of Loc Ninh

Earlier, I wrote about my frustration with the strategy of engaging the enemy and finally securing a piece of terrain only to abandon it later. We almost always won the battles over previously won land, but sustained new causalities retaking the same ground. This type of warfare was perplexing and challenging.

Oh, I remember now—this cyclic seize-and-surrender strategy was all about increasing enemy body count. Amazing how we never seemed to run out of bad guys to fight. I guess the enemy had more soldiers than the Military Assistance Command Vietnam (MACV) or the "big picture" decision-makers in Washington realized. Or maybe it just didn't matter. Our policies were unchangeable, and body counts for both the enemy and the US would continue to mount.

To illustrate my point, Loc Ninh was a key battleground throughout the Vietnam War. History shows there were many battles fought between the US Army and the North Vietnamese Army regulars. I was at the first battle of Loc Ninh, which was the largest military operation for my unit during my tour of duty. Two battalions from the 1st Brigade, 1st Infantry Division—my battalion included—were sent to reinforce an ARVN (South Vietnamese Army) force that was protecting the city. The mission lasted for about six weeks from late October to early December.

Loc Ninh is a town located in Binh Long province, a few miles east of the Cambodian border and about seventy miles northwest of Saigon. It was a hotly contested area because of Loc Ninh's proximity to Cambodia, which made it the perfect spot for staging North Vietnamese troops. Staging troops there was a smart military tactic because our rules of engagement expressly prohibited us from entering Cambodia.

The enemy troops who fought in the TET offensive in January 1968 planned their attacks and organized their combat assault units in Cambodia. From Cambodia and Laos, NVA and Viet Cong could attack units of the Big Red One and quickly retreat back into Cambodia, knowing we could not pursue them.

Loc Ninh is located on major routes leading directly into Saigon, the South Vietnam capital. Thus, this province was a strategic and valuable piece of real estate. The jungle terrain made it a great place for the NVA and Viet Cong to establish and conceal their base camps. And so, they did. They had years to prepare massive, complex underground facilities complete with hospitals, kitchens, ammo storage and sleeping wards. These encampments were difficult to detect and provided cover from our ever-persistent aerial surveillance flights and subsequent bombing missions.

It was late in the year, and the enemy was bringing in soldiers from across the Cambodian border on a large scale. US intelligence identified this large-scale buildup around Loc Ninh, and the generals sent us in to do something about it. There were thousands of enemy combatants. Wow, we knew this was big stuff. However, we knew the area well, were a highly skilled fighting force and had a job to do. Everyone knew it was going to be an active and very dangerous month.

During this period, we discovered how uplifting it was to work with scout dogs for the first time. The dogs I buddied-up with on patrols were German Shepherds. They were extremely well-trained and unconditionally protective of their handler. Their incredible noses could sniff out danger at great distances—booby traps, underground ammo dumps, a base camp or an enemy soldier/sniper waiting in ambush. Such an ability gave our patrol a decided advantage in the jungle.

When these four-legged warriors sensed something out of the ordinary, they'd signal their handlers. It didn't take us long to learn a valuable combat lesson—when a scout dog went on alert, so did we. It was best to have the dog near the front of the patrol so it could alert the point man to danger. However, walking point made the handler and the dog more vulnerable to incoming enemy fire.

The dog handlers I met were very brave men whose job was to search for hazards. On the other hand, I was happy to avoid danger at all costs. One handler and his scout dog were killed while working with our company. To their everlasting credit, their sacrifices saved many other GI lives.

To begin this large-scale operation, we air-assaulted into the Loc Ninh area and established a night defensive perimeter. The chopper ride was uneventful. There was no hostile fire, but evidence of the enemy was easy to spot. The jungle trails were well-worn, and we detected several sniper and ambush positions that were under construction.

We figured we'd be at this location for a week or two, so we dug our bunkers a little deeper and put an extra layer of sandbags on the roof—more protection from enemy rockets and mortars. Having the ability to get below ground was essential when you are in the infantry and subject to attack.

Just after dark, we came under enemy attack. Over the next week, these intrusions were nightly occurrences. Fortunately, they were mostly harassments as opposed to full-scale attacks. Surprisingly, we did not sustain any combat injuries from these frequent disruptions. Like good soldiers, we followed Army protocol and made sure our bunkers were well-built and our fire zones clear.

God definitely protected us from the airborne mortar and rocket evils of the VC. We did not suffer any nighttime casualties that first week, at least for my platoon. Over the next few days, we executed several search and destroy patrols around the NDP and frequently engaged the enemy in minor skirmishes. Again, no serious casualties occurred in my platoon.

One night, however, we heard a ferocious firefight erupt in the distance. Around three o'clock that morning, we received orders to move out toward the village of An Loc, where a nearby Special Forces compound was under heavy attack and needed support fast. We "saddled up" and headed to the fight, reaching the compound just before sun-up to begin a counter-attack on the retreating NVA forces.

We secured the Special Forces compound without suffering any casualties. The same couldn't be said for the Special Forces and ARVN defenders. They had been hit hard. Our counter-assault role changed to perimeter security and mop-up. Medical aid was already in play, and the injured were being evacuated. *Lucky me, no triage this night.*

I recall being totally exhausted from the quick march to support this camp and the extensive release of adrenaline. Unfortunately, we became exposed to the remnant of a human wave attack.

As we neared the defensive perimeter of the compound, I will never forget the sight I came upon. Countless civilian bodies were entangled in the concertina wire surrounding the camp. It was the first time I witnessed the carnage caused by the heartless NVA use of civilians as shields in a human wave attack. They had force-marched the inhabitants of a small village nearby into the compound's direct line of fire.

In theory, the NVA believed, these unwilling civilian combatants would shield them from American and ARVN firepower. Innocent women, children and old people were caught in a hailstorm of bullets and needlessly killed. In the darkness, confusion and chaos dictated the inevitable outcome. The American Special Forces had no choice but to shoot the civilians so they could target the enemy soldiers. Overhead flares exposed numerous bodies caught in the wire. It made me sick. I now hated the NVA and Viet Cong more than ever because of their chicken shit disregard for civilian human life. I noted that several of the civilians had been shot in the back.

The next morning, my platoon was sent on a patrol to pursue the enemy that had attacked the compound the previous night. As we stealthily moved through the brush, we could hear small skirmishes erupting throughout the valley, so we knew we were in for another tough day. We were on high alert, paying close attention to every noise and movement around us. Every soldier exercised extra caution.

At the sound of the skirmishes, we went into stealth mode, which meant no noise and no smoking. We walked in column spaced about five yards apart. As we followed our pre-determined route, artillery shells were fired over our heads every few minutes to confuse the enemy and disrupt any potential ambushes.

Our platoon leader and the forward operation coordinator (FOC) were in constant communication with a nearby battery of 105 howitzers. The FOC was responsible for calling in artillery fire. When necessary, the FOC would coordinate the various aircraft attacking the enemy's firing positions. This skillful lieutenant was very good at his job and always knew our precise coordinates on the map. He had his own radio operator and was continuously in contact with both the artillery battery and the support aircraft assigned to fly air cover for our patrol area of operation.

For this patrol, the artillery was ordered to shoot high explosive rounds that would land about a hundred yards to our front and flanks. This procedure was protocol and usually effective, but it was not free from risk. Listening to rounds whistling over your head is very scary. Here's why. During our patrol that day, I had heard a "clunk" instead of the familiar "whoosh-thump" of a round exiting the cannon.

As seasoned veterans, we knew a clunk meant it was going to be a short round, which is a very bad thing. They are called "short rounds" because they usually fell short of the intended target. Upon hearing the clunk, like a group of talented acrobats, we immediately dove for the ground in unison and pulled our helmet straps extra tight. Within moments, that short-round landed amidst our patrol and detonated.

Some soldiers were only ten feet from the blast. With a loud flash and boom, dirt and projectile fragments were hurled into the air.

Amazingly, this 105mm short round blew apart into three big chunks that flew upward and outward. According to the principals of physics in combat, these types of shells are designed to explode up and out, not down and sideways. We were very lucky once again to dodge injury. Soldiers know that lying prone on the ground lessens the chance of becoming a casualty when bombs or grenades explode.

It never ceased to amaze me how many dangerous positions the Army put us in. *Let's just say it was one more close call.* I wondered how many close calls I could survive before my luck ran out.

Shortly after that incident, a major battle erupted east of our location. Two of our sister companies were ambushed by an NVA regiment and quickly engaged in a gruesome firefight. That enemy regiment was the one we were searching for, but before we could surprise them, they had ambushed our cohorts. Historical records later revealed that an enemy regiment of five hundred soldiers had fought our guys that day. They had set up an ambush shaped like an "L" at the edge of a clearing. Our forces were moving through a rubber plantation and stopped just short of the clearing. The NVA regulars were well dug in and had placed dozens of snipers in the trees, which allowed them to concentrate maximum firepower on our troops.

Summoned to help, our platoon cast caution to the wind and double-timed to the battle. We were not afraid—we were pissed off. Radio traffic had detailed the severity of the battle, and we knew there were casualties. I cannot fully describe our exhilaration as we rushed like John Wayne to the aid of our brothers. We could tell by the sounds of battle that this was a massive and vicious firefight.

We covered the five hundred yards to our comrades in about fifteen minutes, which is extremely good time for travel through thick jungle. Bodies from both sides were everywhere, and the sound of mop-up fire and counter-attacks still raged. The cries of human suffering and the odors of battle announced the gravity of the situation before I could see it. The air was thick with smoke and the stench of death. Blown-up bunkers and broken trees bore witness to the carnage.

Our rage turned into shock as we realized the extent of the destruction. Nearly 100 percent of our battalion command structure had been killed or wounded. The initial burst of gunfire from the ambush, always the deadliest, because of the element of surprise, had killed the battalion commanding officer, Colonel Stigall. Snipers had tied themselves into the trees, which allowed them to keep firing after they were hit. The enemy had also emerged from spider-holes that had carefully concealed their presence. Dead bodies were everywhere. Enemy soldiers were littered among our fellow soldiers.

At a recent First Infantry Division Society Reunion, I sat at a table with two soldiers from Company B, which had taken the brunt of the firefight that day. I told them I was in the rescue force that came to support and mop up. They both thanked me and said how relieved they were when we came charging to the rescue. "It was a sight we would never forget," one of them told me. They remarked about how we had come in hell-bent for a fight with the NVA. We didn't creep into the area; we *charged* in to help our brothers. It was a fairly long battle, but as usual, most of the wounding and killing took place in the first ten minutes.

Our platoon provided flanking fire to eliminate any remaining insurgents. We began cutting down trees to create a landing zone for dust-offs for the killed and wounded. For the most part, other medics already had addressed the initial needs of the wounded. The triage area had been established, and casualties prioritized according to their likelihood of survival. I treated a few less severely injured soldiers and helped with the many dust-off evacuations.

I also gave some moral support to the other medics. Their efforts had been heroic, indeed. They were exhausted and out of supplies. The rubber plantation was dense, so we had to cut down trees to make room for medivacs to land. This process would take hours. The medics all worked their asses off that day and saved a lot of lives.

For the survivors, the time after battle is always spent reliving what had just happened and letting the adrenaline complete its natural cycle, which usually left them exhausted.

Every November 7, I think about that battle and how it went down. While we were advancing toward the chaos, I had been very nervous about going into battle and tried to mentally prepare myself for the bloodbath and the casualties. I knew a lot of brothers were in a world of hurt. These were not the normal thoughts of a young man of twenty years. But I knew I was part of a very noble profession, that I had been in that situation before, and that I would be again.

Sadly, our popular battalion commander, LTC Stigall, was one of those brave souls killed that day. His heroic actions earned him the Army Distinguished Service Cross, the second-highest medal for valor. His DSC citation reads, "The President of the United States of America, authorized by Act of Congress, July 9, 1918 (amended by act of July 25, 1963), takes pride in presenting the Distinguished Service Cross (Posthumously) to Lieutenant Colonel (Infantry) Arthur Donald Stigall (ASN: 0-69805), United States Army, for extraordinary heroism in connection with military operations involving conflict with an armed hostile force in the Republic of Vietnam, while serving with Headquarters and Headquarters Company, 1st Battalion, 26th Infantry, 1st Infantry Division. Lieutenant Colonel Stigall distinguished himself by exceptionally valorous actions on 7 November 1967 while leading two of his infantry companies on a search-and-destroy mission near Loc Ninh. Moving through an abandoned rubber plantation, his entire force was suddenly subjected to intensely savage claymore mine detonations, small arms, and automatic weapons fire from a numerically superior Viet Cong force. Both companies sustained heavy casualties in the initial moments of the attack by the well-concealed enemy.

"Colonel Stigall positioned his command post between the two companies and established maximum control of the defensive actions of his troops. His position was then subjected to vicious fire and he was shot through the knee. Courageously ignoring his wound, he initiated skillful, determined counter-fire against the enemy. When he received word that one of his company commanders had been wounded, he immediately assumed the direction of that company by radio. Enemy fire destroyed his radio and he repeatedly exposed himself to the ravaging hostile fire to direct his troops by voice as he searched for another radio. An exploding Viet Cong rocket knocked him to the ground. He again stood up in the deadly hail of fire, and when he saw a radio operator nearby, he ran toward his position, firing at the advancing enemy with his pistol until he received a mortal wound. His continual display of courage and determination was responsible for his mens' coordinated and effective reaction to the insurgent attack and undoubtedly saved many of his comrades' lives. Lieutenant Colonel Stigall's extraordinary heroism and devotion to duty, at the cost of his life, were in keeping with the highest traditions of the military service and reflect great credit upon himself, his unit, and the United States Army."

This is exactly what men do in combat without personal regard for their own safety. He displayed his leadership and bravery. We all liked that guy because he was a soldier's soldier. He went on patrol in the bush with us even though he did not have to be there. He wanted to lead from the front and was a great inspiration to us all. We were proud to have him as our leader and saddened by his death.

Specialist Stryker, a grenadier in Company C, was also killed that day. He was awarded the Congressional Medal of Honor. His citation reads, "For conspicuous gallantry and intrepidity at the risk of his life above and beyond the call of duty. Sp4c. Stryker, US Army, distinguished himself while serving with Company C. Sp4c. Stryker was serving as a grenadier in a multi-company reconnaissance in force near Loc Ninh. As his unit moved through the dense underbrush, it was suddenly met with a hail of rocket, automatic weapons and small arms fire from enemy forces concealed in fortified bunkers and in the surrounding trees. Reacting quickly, Sp4c. Stryker fired into the enemy positions with his grenade launcher. During the devastating exchange of fire, Sp4c. Stryker detected enemy elements attempting to encircle his company and isolate it from the main body of the friendly force. Undaunted by the enemy machine gun and small-arms fire, Sp4c. Stryker repeatedly fired grenades into the trees, killing enemy snipers and enabling his comrades to sever the attempted encirclement. As the battle continued, Sp4c. Stryker observed several wounded members of his squad in the killing zone of an enemy claymore mine. With complete disregard for his safety, he threw himself upon the mine as it was detonated. He was mortally wounded as his body absorbed the blast and shielded his comrades from the explosion. His unselfish actions were responsible for saving the lives of at least 6 of his fellow soldiers. Sp4c. Stryker's great personal bravery was in keeping with the highest traditions of the military service and reflects great credit upon himself, his unit, and the US Army."

The Army further recognized his heroism by naming the Stryker Assault Vehicle in his honor. I learned of the complete stories of these two men only recently when I visited the First Infantry Division Museum. It is painful for me fifty years later to reflect upon that day. This battle was simply one more illustration that soldiers did their job to the utmost of their ability.

Having witnessed the aftermath and having talked to those tired and weary combatants, that day will be forever seared in my memory. In retrospect, November 7, 1967, taught me the true meaning of bravery and what the human battle spirit can do when pushed to the limits. Coming to the aid of these brave men, men who unhesitatingly gave their all for the benefit of their brothers, is truly a humbling experience.

I remember how we all felt about the devastation to our Blue Spader Battalion and our leaders. They were good soldiers and good men. We respected them all because they were in the field and on patrol with us.

It would take a while for Company B and Company C to rebuild. My company, Company A, would have to do a little more lifting for the foreseeable future. Just one more minor challenge along the path to our date of departure from Vietnam.

The after-action reports listed fifteen Americans killed in action and more than twenty-five wounded. The NVA sustained ninety-three killed and hundreds more wounded. The North Vietnamese regiment made the mistake of withdrawing across an open field to be greeted by Huey and Cobra gunships with rockets and machine guns. The F-4 Phantom jets that arrived on scene from another mission were out of bombs but did have plenty of bullets left in their on-board air arsenal. They attacked the enemy with 20 mm cannon fire. The NVA forces were annihilated. This was one of the few times that we got to apply immediate combat retaliatory justice in force. In most previous circumstances, the enemy simply vanished after ambushing our patrols. While this NVA regiment was severely thrashed, their beating came at great human cost to our Blue Spaders battalion.

A few years ago, I cried while watching a public television program about the "War in Vietnam." There, on screen, a reporter conducted an interview with the NVA commander in charge of the forces who had ambushed our boys that fateful day. The interview was surreal and caused me to flashback to the unforgettable events of that day. There, in the safety of my own living room, I found myself reliving that battle-filled afternoon again. The same emotions I had experienced backfilled my body once more.

That one large-scale battle was the conclusion of the many search-and-destroy patrols and firefights executed by all units during those few days. The "Battle for Loc Ninh After Action Operations Report" indicated that the communist losses during those few days were significant with estimated dead ranging from eight-hundred-fifty to just over a thousand. These extensive battle losses forced the enemy to retreat into Cambodia, where they regrouped and began rearming for the TET Offensive in early 1968. We would face this regiment of enemy soldiers again.

Chapter 23

TET 1968

How lucky can a guy get? Right after our historically significant field trip to Loc Ninh, I received orders to go on R&R for a week. The anguish and fatigue caused by numerous firefights weighed heavily on all of us. Lots of death and destruction on countless patrols and nighttime ambush missions had left me physically and emotionally exhausted. I was more than ready to faithfully discharge my temporary duty as a "soldier on vacation," and to the maximum extent possible, I was going to enjoy myself.

So, I dutifully boarded the daily field supply chopper for our base camp in Quan Loi. Then I packed my ditty bag and boarded a 123 fixed-winged aircraft for Ton Son Nhut Airport in Saigon. *Whoopie!* As fate would have it again, I was in the air on January 30, 1968, and en route to Japan when the TET offensive began. I was a couple thousand miles away from my unit, which was now in the midst of rebuffing the enormous North Vietnamese surge.

After arriving in Tokyo and processing through military customs, I was told to check in daily with the provost sergeant to find out if I would be ordered back to my unit. *Right!* Well, I did the daily check-in thing but caught a break after two days when I was told to enjoy myself for the remainder of my visit.

Now that this matter was settled, I began to enjoy my vacation. I toured museums, the centers of cultural and historically significant memorials. Well, in all honesty, I did not really visit that many noteworthy institutions unless I include several local bars and family-owned restaurants. I did visit a pagoda and took the tram up to Mount Fuji. I also spent one evening exploring the city with a friend from Indiana. He was stationed with the Air Force in Japan. He proudly served as my tour guide to a few more interesting but less culturally significant sites that catered to the interests of the American soldier.

My dad had wired some "good time" money to my hotel. He fully understood the need for this soldier to have a good time because he instinctively knew about the shit that was awaiting my return in Vietnam. During my local adventures, I was amazed to discover that Japanese performers could sing all of the popular GI songs of the time with a perfect American accent.

I enjoyed sleeping in a hotel bed and watching episodes of *Gunsmoke* starring Sheriff Matt Dillon on Japanese television. I couldn't understand what a Japanese-speaking Sheriff Dillon was saying, but I sure enjoyed his sense of justice and his lusty admiration for Ms. Kitty. I knew the storyline and that he would defeat the bad guys—just like we were doing in Vietnam, or so I thought.

I also spent a considerable amount of time flushing the toilet. Why? Because I could! I hadn't seen or used one of those household devices in a long time. It was nice to be surrounded by normality instead of confusion and abnormality, even if people didn't speak English. I visited a tailor and had some silk shirts made as well as a couple of nice suits. *Man, I looked good in those civilian duds.* I sent them home to St. Paul along with a Sony tape recorder for my dad. Too bad the clothes ceased to fit a month after I got out of the Army, and my body realigned to a civilian girth.

On February 6, I boarded a plane back to Saigon. I can't say my batteries were totally re-charged, but the experience was memorable. This R&R had come at the perfect time in my combat adventure. The return flight was noteworthy because we were the first plane to land in Saigon since the TET Offensive had begun.

Everyone, including the pilots, was worried about a rocket attack on our transport. You could see bomb craters near the airport runway. I was relieved when we touched down without any incident. My combat instincts went back on full alert during the bus ride to our heliport several miles away in Bien Hoa.

The bus, with no armed escorts and just one MP with an M-16 in the front seat, entered Saigon and drove down the main road. I witnessed several firefights down some of the side streets and felt extremely vulnerable because I had no weapons and no aid bag should the need arise.

Finally, I arrived back at Bien Hoa and promptly jumped aboard a helicopter to return to my unit in the field. The well-documented TET Offensive continued throughout the month of February. My unit was dispatched to the Michelin Rubber Plantation. We must have worked that plantation at least twelve times in the past six months. We'd capture the terrain, then retreat and give it back for the enemy to reoccupy so we could re-take the plantation once again and then... How crazy was that?

Recent intelligence reports indicated the plantation was prime hunting grounds for enemy troops. We found several enemy basecamps there, but the enemy was not interested in engaging. They had been beaten up pretty badly because of their failed attempt to take Saigon during the first couple days of TET. At least one NVA division was moving through to regroup in Cambodia.

Our battalion executed many patrols, but they produced little contact with the NVA. Although my company did experience a few skirmishes, I did not have to treat any significant wounds. We were certainly not disappointed with this uneventful two-week operation. Our commanders might have been frustrated because no major battles occurred, but they did not work us overtime. The mission would be one of the few times "Army management" did not receive complaints from the grunts about the operation. We called it easy duty. Both the enemy and our battle-hardened unit lived to fight another day.

During TET, Ho Chi Minh sent several thousand enemy troops into South Vietnam. Subsequently, major battles erupted throughout the country. North Vietnam's military goal was to attack and capture every provincial capital that would, in their way of thinking, cause the populace to revolt against the South Vietnamese government and join the resistance effort. This was their big push to defeat the ARVN military and force the Americans to withdraw from the war. These well-executed, countrywide, head-to-head attacks resulted in significant battle losses for the ARVNs and the US but were disastrous for the NVA and Viet Cong.

The NVA and VC ran smack into the jaws of our far superior military firepower and suffered greatly for it. Both the US Army and the ARVN Army soundly defeated the NVA and Viet Cong in every battle. So ruinous was the overall defeat, historical records tell us it took Hanoi two years to rebuild their force. Throughout the remainder of 1968, however, the enemy did rebuild and once again pressed their agenda. We all know how the story ended.

Chapter 24

Ambush in the Binh Dong Bush

Near the end of February, we participated in a company-sized patrol in Binh Dong Province. Our search-and-destroy patrols had increased in frequency after the initial TET Offensive. We were still pursuing a beat-up and short-handed enemy that was intent on fleeing to Cambodia to regroup. Our unit served as a blocking force, which meant we spent a lot of time thrashing about in very dense jungle.

On this particular day, we were on patrol a few miles from Dian, which was a regional South Vietnamese province capital and 1st Infantry Division headquarters. Suddenly, all hell broke loose, and we came under heavy attack from the left flank. The whole world seemed to erupt around us, and the typically organized chaos of a major firefight began. Gunsmoke and loud explosions came from everywhere. As usual, my heart jumped, and I went on full alert. I dove to the ground positioned for battle. So did everyone else.

By now, my actions were automatic. I knew what to expect—but in combat, the flow of events is never routine. You learn to expect the unexpected, which can lead to some creative battle solutions.

In the initial burst of enemy gunfire, one of the flank guards was killed and another seriously wounded with a life-threatening head injury that needed my attention ASAP. But he was pinned down by an enemy sniper who was in a nearby tree who fired at him whenever he moved. His screams pierced the dense jungle cover. Nothing can get your juices flowing like an injured soldier shouting for the medic.

The shouts always meant high stress and extreme danger, but also served as a signal for me, the problem-solver medic, to get to work. I had to leave the relative safety of my prone position and make a house call in a dangerous part of town. I couldn't wait for all hostiles to be eliminated, so I made my move, insisting that the M-60 machine gunner escort me to provide covering fire as I administered emergency first aid.

In a situation like this, flank guards and the point man are typically fifteen to twenty yards away from the main column on patrol. The flank and point soldiers were the bait in our patrol's trap. These unfortunate lads were the most vulnerable to an enemy attack. They had two of the most dangerous job in the Army.

Their jobs were to detect the enemy by their movement and break up any potential ambushes. Their actions protected the main column from sneak attack, thus the "bait" reference. This technique was highly successful. Unfortunately, these individuals were the first soldiers to engage the enemy and the first ones to get killed or wounded. On this day, this formation technique worked as was designed, and the flank guards made the initial contact.

My newly appointed machine-gun-toting bodyguard helped execute our rescue plan. This machine gun specialist was a stout-hearted fellow with an intense disposition. He was a dependable, rock-solid warrior with abundant courage, plus he was very good with the M-60 machine gun. I knew him well and trusted his ability to cover my ass. He had played that role in previous firefights.

Very cautiously, we low-crawled to the injured flank guards. Bullets were whizzing everywhere, but thankfully missing us. I could never figure out how that happened. I remember the noise, the smoke, the smell of combat, and bracing myself for the arrival of an enemy grenade. Fortunately, no grenade found us.

My fearless partner went to work making his M-60 spit fire with deadly accuracy. As the machine gunner laid down cover fire in the bush and in the trees, I finish crawling to the first injured soldier and found him dead. I said a brief prayer and tendered his care to the Lord. Just a few feet away, however, lay a man I could help. He was alive but in a state of panic and a world of hurt. I told him to remain still.

On patrol with the M-60 machine gun. That's some real firepower.

At this point, concealment was our best option to avoid further injury and to give time for the M-60 gunner to get the upper hand in this battle. I clearly remember the sound of that M-60 spitting fire and causing bamboo brush and tree limbs to fall to the ground—pure devastation combined with the sweet smell of friendly fire. No enemy within range could survive the deadly ferocity of an M-60 in the hands of an expert marksman. And none did.

When the incoming firing stopped, I rolled my wounded companion onto his back and saw the extent of his severe injuries. Next, I grabbed his harness and asked him to lift his head so I could pull him to safety. I dragged him to better cover so I could administer first aid. Fortunately for us, my machine gun superhero killed several snipers who had tied themselves into the trees above us. His actions saved my life and prevented further injury or death to our already seriously wounded brother. Like most M-60 operators, he was an unsung hero that day.

My battle-wounded warrior was a real pal to all of us, a happy-go-lucky fellow who was good at his job and cared about protecting his brothers. When others were told to take the flank or point position and they hesitated, he frequently volunteered. He had a keen alertness for danger, so we were happy when he was on the job. Regrettably, it is almost impossible to protect yourself when you unknowingly walk into an ambush with a tree-clinging, camouflaged sniper as your assassin.

The sniper's bullet hit him on the left side of his head and face above the ear. It was a damaging blow that traveled in a downward direction. The AK-47 bullet took out his left eye. All that remained was a hollow hole where the eye used to be. The bullet continued across his face and cut a swath through the bridge of his nose and shattered the cheekbone and eye socket just beneath his right eye. The damage was severe, and his right eye was dangling out of the socket. *Now what the hell do I do? We didn't train for this in school either.*

I needed to place his eye back in the socket, then address the injuries to both eyes and dress his massive wound. I thought a wet compression bandage was better than a dry one because I wanted the surgeons to be able to remove my dressing without further damaging his already critical wound. In dealing with such a massive trauma in the field, I couldn't worry about infection. I knew the hospital had drugs to address that threat.

I took a couple of 4 x 4 gauze bandages and wet them with water from my canteen. I placed the remaining eye, which was still attached to the optic cord, gently back into the socket and wrapped his entire head with the wet bandages. An Ace elastic bandage held everything in place. Interestingly, he was not in much pain and was quite lucid. There was not a lot of bleeding, but I needed to get him out of there as fast as I could.

With my heart still pounding, I took a few deep breaths to help gather my wits. Because of the brush, I knew I couldn't carry him on my back or on my portable stretcher. He couldn't see, but he was mobile, so I got him to his feet and told him to hang onto the webbing of my utility belt. Moving very slowly, we walked to relative safety at the rear of our column, where there was a clearing large enough to bring in a dust-off. The soldier hung onto my belt and carefully followed. The evacuation point was about a hundred yards away.

As in other situations, we exchanged very few words that day. Although he knew he was badly injured, I offered encouragement and assured him he would survive.

A dust-off soon touched down and transported him to a nearby MASH unit. He survived his ordeal, but I learned that he eventually lost the eye I tried to save. I've always wondered what more I could have done to save that eye.

I do remember how nervous I felt at the time. I was drenched with sweat from the adrenaline rush. My ten weeks of combat medic training had not prepared me for situations like this. This soldier would survive the war but face life as another blind combat veteran. The sacrifices of a few truly benefit so many, another example of the price some people have paid to help us remain free.

It's remarkable, I think, that I can recall every detail of that day as if it happened yesterday. War does that to a person because these traumatic experiences are always alive within us. The real challenge is trying to figure out how to deal with them.

Shortly after the dust-off headed to the trauma hospital, the firefight erupted again. Instinctively, I dove over a berm for protection. To my embarrassment, I rolled directly on top of our company commander. Typically, a company commander in an infantry unit holds the rank of captain, but in this case, our excellent leader was a major. He was taking his turn leading our company so he could get the combat experience he needed to advance as a professional soldier.

Becoming skilled in combat is a sure way to get promoted in rank. The catch was that you needed to survive the experience.

I was still drained from my flank casualty experience, and the major did a good job helping me refocus on the other tasks at hand. When an adrenaline rush subsides, exhaustion takes over and a twenty-minute timeout is immensely helpful. The major's words of encouragement and his praise for my job were very much appreciated.

Before volunteering for a combat job in Vietnam, the major was a football coach at West Point. He was a master at providing direction and leading young men. I respected the hell out of that guy. We all did. He was smart and had guts and compassion. To survive the rigors of war, I realized we needed to count on the military smarts of our leaders. Most of them rose to the occasion and performed superbly under the most stressful circumstances. I was fortunate to serve under some very fine men.

According to some enlisted Army thinkers, a draftee was a low-life bottom feeder. Regular Army personnel enlisted for a three-year hitch and were much higher on the respect chain because they had made a conscious decision the join the Army. They were willing participants who asked to be put in harm's way as opposed to those of us who were unwilling draftees, even though we ended up being put in harm's way.

On that sultry and excitement-filled afternoon, the major told me he was going to make me the senior medic for the company. That meant I would be promoted to the rank of Enlisted 5 (E-5). The promotion was unexpected but welcomed. While thanking him for this field promotion, I did inform him quite emphatically, "Even though I appreciate your confidence, it doesn't mean I'm going to reenlist for another hitch in the Army."

He smiled and said I was unofficially doing the job of senior aidman anyway, which is an E-5 slot, so I might as well get the pay and the rank. *Wahoo! I would now make a whopping $245 a month including my $65 combat pay.*

I would be taking over the medical responsibility for the entire company. All in all, I felt up to the challenge and looked forward to moving into the headquarters platoon and receiving a little more money. As an aside, the only E-5 slot available in the battalion was a motor pool sergeant, so I became a "hard striper" sergeant instead of a Specialist 5, a rare move in the Army that I thought was very cool.

With the coming of spring came new military strategies to address the lessons learned during the TET Offensive. The war continued, and our unit was once again deployed to the Cambodian border to serve as a blocking force that would deny the enemy an avenue of retreat to their safe havens. As Yogi Berra once said, "It's like déjà vu all over again." We couldn't believe we were back in the same area, fighting new battles against the same soldiers we had fought two months before. We understood the strategy, but it still seemed nonsensical to us simple-minded grunts.

Amazingly, during the next several weeks, I did not have to take care of any human casualties. I said *human* on purpose because I did have an experience of a different kind late one night. We were dug in near a small hamlet in an agricultural area. Our company was safely in position and secure for the night. I was with one of the platoons guarding the perimeter. We were working with a mechanized unit that included a tank and several armored personnel carriers, heavy armament strategically deployed amongst the infantry platoons on the perimeter. I knew I was going to sleep well this night because I was surrounded by a lot of American firepower that could easily repel any enemy ground attacks. We had many .50 caliber machine guns and mobile artillery, not just rifles.

I was positioned next to the tank, which was equipped with a new battle instrument called a "starlight" scope. The tank commander offered me a tour of his armored chariot and demonstrated the new device that used the stars and moon as a light source to project images onto a television monitor. The scope gave you the advantage of specifically knowing where the enemy was located compared to your own position. While it detected movement, this early technology frequently portrayed images that were blurry and confusing rather than well-defined. It was the first generation of such equipment, but we were glad to have it around. Much better than trying to use the naked eye in the dark.

Shortly after midnight, this new wonder scope technology revealed significant movement about three hundred yards in front of the tank. Rather than having the tank shoot at the target, the company commander decided to use the mortar platoon to fire white phosphorous mortar rounds to disrupt the enemy who was sneaking toward us. He did not want to give the tank's position away too soon because he knew the tank would then become the focal point for concentrated enemy fire.

Obeying the commander's instructions, the mortar crew began lobbing rounds at the target. No return fire came back, so the order was given to ceasefire. All movement appeared to be moving quickly away from our position. *Guess we showed them. Hooyah!*

The next morning, we did a sweep of the area to look for enemy bodies and weapons. Imagine our surprise when we came across a herd of confused Holsteins milling around and eating grass. A quick search also revealed the effectiveness of the mortar rounds. We discovered several dead animals that were already starting to decompose in heat and humidity that greeted us each day.

The company commander discovered a surviving Holstein suffering from a phosphorous burn to its buttocks. A piece of phosphorous had landed on the top rear of the cow and left severely burnt flesh.

The captain, being a practical, fiscally conservative man, called me over and said, "Doc, patch up that cow because it'll cost the US government five hundred dollars in reparations if it dies."

Recalling my dad's advice to always follow orders, I set out to address the battle injury on my fifteen-hundred-pound, loudly complaining casualty. I poured Merthiolate in the burned-out hole on the cow's rear and applied a battle dressing. It was a challenge keeping the dressing positioned topside while trying to tie the dressing's strings on the belly of the beast. I thought it was utter nonsense for me to be treating a cow, but I did. I never got a report, though, on whether the Holstein survived.

Once again, I accomplished my combat medic task. I teased the captain and asked if I should call in a dust-off for the white-spotted patient. My professional opinion was that the rescue chopper would have to be a two-bladed Chinook because a Huey couldn't handle such a large load. The captain mumbled something about not being funny, and if the Army had wanted me to have a sense of humor, it would have issued me one.

My handiwork was complete, and the captain was satisfied. We had saved US taxpayers five hundred bucks if you didn't include the five thousand dollars in ordnance we used to create the bovine casualty. So, it was a good day. I can only conclude, "If the Army had wanted me to think, they would have issued me an olive drab brain."

The important take-away to be added to my OJT portfolio that day was "on-the-job military medical training, including the practice of veterinary medicine." Two legs or four, if you were wounded in my presence, I was going to patch you up. Fortunately, for me and the animal kingdom, that was my one and only experience treating a non-human causality of war.

Chapter 25

The War Continues

Sometime in early March, we were sent on a new type of mission. My unit, Blue Spader Company A, was sent to the Mekong Delta to perform search-and-destroy missions while serving aboard an Army Patrol Boat Riverine (PBR). This was a totally new experience for us grunts. These boats were twenty-eight feet long, made of fiberglass and metal, and were very maneuverable and fast. They had twin .50 caliber machine guns pointing forward and a couple of M-60 machine guns covering the flanks.

Riding along the river on a sunny afternoon sounded great. Being from Minnesota, I've always enjoyed the water. Hell, man, maybe we could "wet a line." It had to beat patrolling the jungles while chopping our way through thick bamboo and fighting creepy crawlers and snipers. As on previous missions since the TET offensive, our new assignment was to prevent invader leftovers from crossing the river into Cambodia.

So, we boarded these boats in squad-size units. Our goal was to simply chill out until something happened. Speed is good, but firepower is even better.

It didn't take us long, however, to realize we were more like sitting ducks in a tin can. The enemy seemed to enjoy hiding along the riverbanks to shoot rockets and RPGs at us, never mind using machine guns and

AK-47 fire to disrupt our water patrol. Fortunately, we had protective armor to hide behind. If we could isolate the enemy, it would be our job to land on the riverbank and execute a short patrol to destroy them. *Ah, so the boats were the bait, and we were the executioners. I get it.*

We did receive incoming enemy fire a few times and became land fighters once again. Generally, but not always, the uncooperative VC knew our operating procedures and got out of the area before we could teach them a lesson. Pretty frustrating for combat troops.

Our river excursion only lasted a few days. We spent nights dug in along the shoreline and pulled guard duty to protect the boats. Interestingly, not one of my guys got shot during this amphibious exercise. I know that a few hostiles were forwarded to the afterlife, so the captain called our efforts a success.

Patrolling the river on a boat can be very dangerous. These fast-moving troop carriers were a magnet for enemy fire. We all discovered what it was like to be the fish in the barrel.

Finally, our fun with the navy ended, and we were consigned back to the bush to patrol areas and terrain more to our liking. At least we had jungle to conceal our physical whereabouts from the enemy. I can't believe that we preferred the jungle crap to the river crap! But then again, it is all crap, and that, in a nutshell, is the infantry experience.

In April of 1968, we were on another battalion-size search-and-destroy operation south of Lai Khe. We established a new night defensive position (NDP) late in the day. At dusk, sporadic fire came from the surrounding woodline, but no one was hit in my sector. At least not yet.

Later that night, all hell broke loose as the perimeter again came under heavy attack. Flares went up, and the entire area was illuminated like it was daytime. One of the Listening Posts (LP) was overrun. This LP was the first alert system located about seventy-five yards from the perimeter. Its job was to detect enemy movement and any possible attack on the night defensive perimeter.

Sadly, the two soldiers in the LP did not have a chance to retreat to safety and were killed as soon as the attack began. Several soldiers in the bunkers nearest the concertina wire that surrounded the perimeter were killed as well. Our casualties mounted as we began returning fire at a very high rate. Our company commander called for air and artillery support. Once the high explosives started falling, it did not take long to gain fire superiority. With this brief lull in the action, I began looking for and treating casualties.

I came across an injured soldier lying in his foxhole near the perimeter. His multiple gunshot wounds were severe, and his breathing was very shallow. Just as I began treating his wounds, he stopped breathing. I immediately sat down on the ground, pulled him onto my lap and started giving him mouth to mouth resuscitation. I shut out the noise of the bullets whizzing by focused on saving this man who I did not even know. Regrettably, that soldier died in my arms, and once again, I felt totally helpless.

While CPR worked in training, it didn't always work in combat. Welcome to the realities of war. I said a little prayer for this soldier and moved on because there was much more work to do.

As the evening progressed, sporadic enemy fire kept coming into our sizable NDP. It was amazing to watch the enemy tracers heading in my direction. They bounced all over the place. I ran from foxhole to foxhole, looking for additional wounded grunts.

In the mayhem, it suddenly occurred to me that I made a good target for some enemy rifleman. Wanting to avoid becoming a casualty myself, I dove for the ground and laid perfectly flat to avoid getting hit. Although low crawling in this sandy environment was safer, it also took a lot more time to move from bunker to bunker. Just as I began to feel secure in the prone position, a slight glancing blow from an enemy bullet knocked off my helmet.

I checked my head and torso for a visible wound or a trickle of blood, which were two sure signs I had just earned a Purple Heart. There was no damage, just frazzled nerves. I specifically remember the moment I realized my helmet had saved me from a life-ending injury. I guess that is why we wore the damn things, uncomfortable as they were. *Not even a scratch.* But I wondered how many close calls I could take before my luck ran out.

Several other medics began to mop up and check the bunkers for casualties. I came across one slightly wounded soldier who was lying prone near the perimeter wire. He had suffered a gunshot wound to his leg, which was easy to treat. Unfortunately for me, he was not mobile. I patched his leg and used the "fireman's carry" to move him to a more secure location.

I remember how easily I accomplished that task. Either I was strong as hell or my adrenaline was doing its job. I think the latter. We practiced the fireman's carry during our training at Fort Sam. I found it to be a highly effective mode of transport, but it made me a slow-moving target for sure. Thank God the enemy did not see me extract my casualty.

Our standard operating procedure was to dispatch several squads at dusk in different directions. These smaller fighting units would set ambushes that were supposed to alert our Night Defensive Position (NDP) to any impending attacks. We all knew these Ambush Patrol (AP) missions were almost suicidal but absolutely necessary. By design, these soldiers were the sacrificial lambs in the process of protecting the battalion's position.

Since it was obvious a sizable enemy force was in the area, it did not come as a surprise to learn that one of our night ambush patrols made heavy contact before they could get into their defensive position. A heavy firefight developed, and the patrol became trapped some seven hundred yards from the NDP. The patrol reported that three soldiers had suffered significant wounds, and one of the casualties was the medic. With only eight men still mobile, there was no way they could care for the wounded and fight their way back to the perimeter on their own.

Because I was the senior medic for Company A, the battalion medical doctor came to me and requested that I send out a rescue team to extract the ambush patrol, which was on the verge of annihilation.

The benefits of having our MD with us on these larger-scale operations were enormous. We could get the wounded into treatment much more quickly than waiting for a dust-off, particularly at night. In any event, the doctor (my boss) asked what I thought I could do about the situation. It was obvious they desperately needed help, and I was now going to be part of the solution. We needed to rescue them as quickly as possible, treat the wounded and extract the patrol back to the relative safety of the perimeter.

I volunteered to lead the medical team for the rapidly organized rescue patrol. I coordinated with the platoon leader who was a lieutenant, and we quickly developed a plan to retrieve the patrol. I told the doctor I wanted to take two other medics with me so we each could treat one casualty. This would save a lot of time once we reached the downed patrol and allow us to get the wounded back to the aid station and the doctor sooner rather than later. He agreed, so I recruited two other medics as hesitant volunteers. In our minds, we all knew it was going to be a very dangerous mission, and the probability of getting killed or injured was great. We had no choice but to do our job. By now, being scared was routine. But, somehow, we always mustered the courage to go to the aid of our brothers.

While time is always critical in taking care of the wounded, a "fast jaunt" to rescue the "shot-up" ambush patrol was not in the cards. As we anticipated, our platoon-sized rescue force had to fight the NVA all along our entire route to the trapped AP. It was just past midnight when we left the safety of the perimeter. The limited moonlight didn't provide much help in lighting our way. Rather, this celestial illumination seemed to create more ghostly shadows in our already overactive minds. It didn't matter because the jungle terrain we traversed was more difficult than any obstacle course I experienced during my Army stateside training. Hills, ditches and downed trees slowed our travel. Our rescue expedition force was also receiving seemingly relentless harassment of enemy fire. The terrain and harassment fire seemingly made it impossible to focus on putting one foot in front of the other. I knew this was going to be a very difficult mission to complete.

True to form, however, we had injured comrades that needed our help, and we would not be deterred. I remembered the First Infantry Division motto: "No mission too difficult. No sacrifice too great. Duty first!" Fear was with us, but we had resolve. We had a job to do, and we kept moving. We had the heart of warriors! Thank God, none of the ghostly shadows that were sniping at our patrol were good shots, and we reached our brothers without any further casualty related incident.

During the chaos, I began to think about our exit strategy once we reached our destination and packed up the wounded. *How in the hell are we going to carry these guys 700 yards on our return trip through this seemingly impossible terrain?* This would surely be an enormous physical and mental challenge. Such an exercise was not in the Army manual or in my training background. We eventually reached our embattled brothers, who were very pleased to see us. However, I knew we were only halfway home in completing our mission. The three wounded combatants needed us to fix 'em up, pack 'em up and get 'em back to the perimeter for an enhanced level of safety and medical treatment.

As soon as we got to the beleaguered patrol, I surveyed the three wounded soldiers and assigned a medic to each one. I began to treat the most seriously injured soldier and desperately tried to start an IV. I tried several times. I tried to put the needle in both arms and even tried to find a vein in his ankle but no luck. He was already in severe shock. I still think about how difficult it was to treat him using a red filtered flashlight as my light source. It seemed an impossible challenge, but by now, the near-impossible became the norm. There were still lots of enemy combatants in the area and sporadic gunfire. I treated his battle injury and somewhat stopped the bleeding. I remember being extremely frustrated about not getting an IV started, but we were very short on time. He desperately needed fluids to replace the large amount of blood he lost. The next best thing was to get all of us the hell out of there before the enemy regrouped and began a new attack on our position.

There would be no helicopter dust-off helping us tonight. It took about thirty minutes to render our emergency medical treatment. We loaded our wounded on rigid stretchers and strapped them down. I was glad I made the decision to bring regular rigid stretchers with us as opposed to relying on the typical canvas jungle stretcher, which we normally used in the field. The far less functional jungle stretcher was flimsy and made it difficult to carry a person very far. The decision to use hard stretchers made it much easier to carry our injured. I don't know if anyone else has ever had to accomplish such a daunting task as carrying wounded comrades as far as we did that night. As we made the return trip back to the safety of the perimeter, we carried our three wounded brothers over hills, through ditches and up over downed trees. As I mentioned before, it was very difficult terrain. The trip was so difficult we had to spell our stretcher bearers several times. Each man in the platoon took a turn. We eventually made it back to the perimeter, where we tendered care to the doctor. It took us three hours to complete this mission. As hard as we tried to save these brave men, the casualty I was treating died. *Just another merciless night in Vietnam!* There would be a lifetime to think about what could have been.

This was the longest night of my life, and the entire time, I was on edge and scared shitless. It was one of the most exhausting and difficult physical and mental things I have ever done. But that's war for you. Always new adventures and personal challenges.

Sometime in late April, we were once again assigned to execute search-and-destroy patrols in the Michelin Rubber Plantation in the Iron Triangle. As in the past, we were to engage any remaining NVA or Viet Cong units that were TET combatants and in the process of regrouping. For this mission, we were assigned to work alongside an armored unit. Because we would be working with tanks and armored personnel carriers (APCs), which always advertised their presence, we knew the enemy would soon find us. Predictably, we ventured into an NVA base camp, and the battle started. I remember lots of RPGs and heavy machine gunfire. I did treat a few minor casualties who were injured by RPG fragments, but all survived and continued the battle task at hand. I sterilized their wounds with Merthiolate (an antiseptic compound), applied some gauze and finished the task by using elastic ace wraps to cover and protect the injury. All of them earned their purple heart, and they now had a story to share with their grandchildren.

As the firefight continued, bullets were flying everywhere, so I took cover on the ground behind one of the tracks of a tank. I felt very smart and perhaps just a little too smug with my choice of cover. While no enemy fire could reach me, I did not factor in the human element. After all, it was a soldier who operated this huge mechanical fighting beast. As rockets started pounding the area in front of the tank, the tank driver was ordered to withdraw. While the tank commander was aware of the order to back up, imagine my surprise that I was not. Once again, I was almost killed as the tank started to back up. Fortunately, I heard the driver shift the tank into reverse. I rolled to the side of the tank, and it missed crushing me by six inches. *What a despicable way to die, getting crushed by one of our own tanks. How would the captain ever explain that in a letter to my mother?* Yet another close call, but once again, I did survive. This incident proves there is really no place that is safe in a war zone.

The battle went on for hours. I treated a few other guys for minor wounds, but nothing catastrophic. I did assist another medic who was dealing with stupidity and injury at the same time. Three of his men, one after another, were shot looking into the same sniper hole adjacent to an underground enemy base camp. They were shooting and dropping hand grenades into the hole in an attempt to kill the enemy soldier guarding the underground entrance. The GI's would shoot and then look into the tunnel entrance. Somehow the enemy sniper was still alive and returned fire resulting in one more GI killed in action. Shoot and get shot. I thought such repeated attempts were crazy and warned two of the eventual victims not to look in the hole but wait for more firepower. This process repeated itself a total of three times until the sergeant wised-up and ordered a tank to be brought forward to remedy the problem. The tank came up, took aim and fired several high explosive rounds into the hole. The results were inconclusive, so the tank then used its flame thrower affectionately called "the zippo." The zippo derived its nickname from the Zippo lighter that we all carried. Our little zippo would light cigarettes; the big zippo would light up the jungle for yards around. The tank operator used the zippo to send a lengthy burst of Napalm into the tunnel. A high explosive round might not make the corners in this tunnel, but the heat from the zippo did. This very nasty instrument of destruction eliminated the threat and the enemy combatants. Unfortunately, three of our men did not need to die this day.

Later that afternoon, I had one of the medics from the armored unit approach me with a heavy request. One of the APCs was hit by an RPG, and the driver was killed. The driver was guiding his track with his hatch open and his head sticking out so he could see better. When they came under fire, he attempted to get his head back inside the hatch for more protection. He did not react quickly enough, and an enemy RPG exploded on his hatch. As a result, his brains were splattered all over the inside of that track. The unit's medic asked me to clean up the human remains stuck to the inside walls of the track because the driver was a very good friend of his, and he was too upset to complete this grueling task. Always one to help a fellow "doc," I grabbed an empty sandbag and collected skull fragments and brain splatter for the next thirty minutes. It was a very hot day, and I still remember the awful smell of cordite and death that compounded the task at hand.

I was respectful of my role, but very sad at the same time. Upon exiting the vehicle, I turned over the contents of my sandbag to the medic. He combined them with the soldier's body, which was already placed in a body bag for the trip back home and eventual burial. Just one more crazy job that needed to be done. No training prepared me for this task either. It was a very hard thing to do, but the other medic deeply appreciated my understanding and assistance. Medics are a compassionate lot, and no task, regardless of the difficulty, shall remain undone. *In combat, you do anything to help a brother.*

Chapter 26

Christmas in the Jungle

The Vietnamese are mostly Buddhists, so Christmas meant nothing special to the Viet Cong or the NVA. For them, the war never really stopped.

On the day before Christmas, we experienced several probes of our night defensive perimeter with a few mortars thrown in as a special holiday gift from an enemy displeased with our presence. Despite these several intrusions, we suffered no casualties. We all hoped that we would be extracted from the field to enjoy the holiday in the comparative safety of our base camp, but that was not to be. Infantry units don't spend time in the rear—we spend time in the unrelenting quest to search out and destroy the enemy.

Alas, this special holiday would be just another combat day in the bush. We already had been out in the field for two weeks, so what's a few more days? After all, we had already prepared some nice combat environs, each day digging our fox holes deeper and stacking more sandbags for added security. We were positioned somewhere in the Iron Triangle, the exact location reserved for those who had maps and needed to know.

Early that morning, the enemy probed our Defensive Position (DP) looking for weak spots in our defenses. We killed a few hostiles but did not suffer any casualties. By this time in my tour, we had experience and some good fortune due, I am sure, to the lessons learned from our "on-the-job training."

After things settled down again, a reconnaissance squad began mopping up the perimeter and captured a few enemy soldiers. I was asked by the company commander to treat a North Vietnamese prisoner of war (POW) who had sustained gunshot wounds to his leg and arm. His injuries were not life-threatening, but like all gunshot wounds, they were quite painful.

I will never forget the look of fear in that man's eyes as I knelt beside him. He began shouting and pulling away. I summoned our interpreter to ask the prisoner what was going on. The prisoner explained that he thought I was the executioner and had come to kill him. Inflicting further harm on this man was the furthest thing from my mind. Another lesson learned.

I guess the NVA regulars and the Viet Cong were just as afraid of being captured by us as we were of being captured by them. Being captured was a major fear factor amongst all soldiers. As combat soldiers do, we speculated on what we'd do if we ever were captured. We contemplated the success of various escape scenarios and concluded there were no good options. It would be best if we all relied on each other to make sure none of us was captured in the first place.

We all had heard rumors about being disemboweled at the hands of enemy captors. We were told that mutilations were a part of war and that some POWs had their penises cut off and shoved in their mouths. The enemy, we'd been told, thought such actions proved they were tough. To us, it proved they were inhumane. Rather than frighten us, these stories pissed us off and steeled our resolve to never get captured.

Fortunately, none of our own troops ever become a POW. Our company did suffer casualties while rescuing a wounded brother, but we never abandoned a downed soldier dead or alive.

Thinking about how to calm the situation with my new POW casualty, I stepped back and lit a cigarette, then put it between his lips. I pulled out my canteen and gave him a drink of water. In a calm voice,

I repeatedly said, "Bac si, bac si," which is Vietnamese for doctor. The despair soon left his face and began to relax. After applying battle dressings to his injuries, he smiled and began thanking me for not killing him as he'd been led to believe would certainly happen.

I smiled back. To me, he was just another casualty caught in the wrong place at the wrong time. I felt no malice towards him, just compassion. I was not the only medic who felt that way. *Guess compassion was part of our Medic DNA.*

My newly treated combatant, however, was not out of the woods. As he was being carried to an ARVN chopper, I grew concerned about his fate. I knew the South Vietnamese soldiers who took the POWs from us were known to throw prisoners out of the helicopter after interrogating them. I asked my interpreter to instruct the ARVN intelligence guys to make sure this man did not experience such a fate. I was told they'd never do such a thing, but I've always wondered if I had saved that man only to let him die at the hands of the ARVNs. *God, I hope not.*

As night descended on this Christmas Eve, a battle erupted a few miles away. Another NDP came under attack and "Puff the Magic Dragon" was asked to make an appearance. This was the first time I witnessed Puff in action. This highly effective gunship was a Douglas AC-47, a two-engine aircraft with three 7.62 mm Gatling mini-guns mounted to its doors. It was a slow-flying plane that could carry one ton of ammunition—54,000 rounds.

This special gunship was designed to provide close air support for ground troops. The rate of fire was 18,000 rounds per minute. The plane could blanket every square foot of a football field in 60 seconds and stay aloft for hours patrolling and protecting US troops. Because of its massive firepower, Puff received its name from the soldiers it protected. Every fifth round was a red tracer. The sum of these rapidly fired, glowing bullets looked like streaks of fire.

To the enemy, Puff breathed fire like a dragon. But to the American soldier, Puff was a great friend. I amazed at the amount of firepower we had available to us in Vietnam.

The battle ended as fast as it had begun, and sleep became the last mission of the day. After the battles of Christmas Eve, we hoped Christmas Day would be more tranquil. Although Christmas was a special event celebrated worldwide, for me, it started out as just another bright, sunny day in the bush.

As a Minnesota boy, it seemed unconscionable to be celebrating Christmas without snow. I missed the soothing voice of Bing Crosby singing *White Christmas*. There were no chestnuts roasting on an open fire in Vietnam and no fake deer antlers on the dog. This would be the first time that I would not be treated to pierogi and kielbasa for supper, as was the tradition passed down by my polish grandparents. *Did I already mention that war is hell?*

After another breakfast of C-rations, I cleaned up our area and readied for the events of the day. Since there would be no patrols on Christmas, I set about to provide some good tidings and thoughts of home. My first job was to erect a small, twelve-inch artificial Christmas tree my mother had sent. Good fortune had fallen upon us because the tree had arrived with my mail a few days before Christmas, surviving the 10,000-mile trip in pristine condition. *What a treat.* I used my bunker as a tree stand. We were surrounded by lots of white sand that reminded me, in a perverted way, of white snow.

With great fanfare and longing memories of all my previous Christmases, I opened my mother's Christmas care package containing cookies, Slim Jim meat sticks, green peppermint gum drops, canned oysters, sardines and crackers. A more perfect gift I could not have imagined. I played a cassette tape I had received from friends in Florida. The recording included several Christmas songs that my foxhole companions and I enjoyed during the holiday lull in the action. We mused about what "real people" were doing on Christmas back in the "real world."

Even though we were in the field, the Army made it a special day, feeding us a wonderful Christmas feast of hot turkey with all the trimmings. Our banquet was delivered by helicopter and served out of mermite food containers. Mermite is an Army term for a cooler that keeps your chow hot. I still remember how wonderful that meal tasted.

As we went through the chow line and stopped at each serving station, the cooks served generous portions of turkey, stuffing, mashed potatoes and gravy, cranberry sauce, yams and buttermilk biscuits. We got our fill of pumpkin pie for dessert. *Man, it was good!*

The last station in the chow line presented a special treat for each soldier—two-ice cold beers served with Christmas good wishes from the battalion commander. That was a first for us, and it was the only time we were ever given beer in the field.

For me, the beer treat soon became even more special. Two of the other medics in my company were Seventh-day Adventists, who were conscientious objectors (COs) and did not drink alcohol. They went through the line, got their alcoholic beverages and then wished me Merry Christmas as they handed me their beers. I was probably the only person that day to have a full six-pack enjoy!

As the day wore on, I grew quite melancholy thinking about how I had never before missed celebrating Christmas with my family. Truthfully, all of us were a bit homesick that day. When I returned to the States, my mother made me promise never to miss Christmas with the family again.

A little piece of sanity from the "world" sent to me by my mother so we could celebrate Christmas in Paradise.

Chapter 27

Village Massacres and Civic Action Patrols

One of my darkest memories of the war was the massacre of civilians who lived in the small village of My Lai. Several hundred old men, women and children were summarily executed at the direction of platoon leader Lt. Calley, Jr., on March 18, 1968. A lot has been written about this "most shocking episode of the Vietnam War." It has been reported that this unsavory part of our military history was an anomaly.

I agree. Sadly, the extensive reporting of this regrettable incident gave rise to the argument that such treatment of civilians was the norm and not the rare exception. Thanks to a cover-up by a few, it took a year before the My Lai Massacre made front-page news. No wonder the public started to lose faith in the truthfulness of our national government. How many more lies were yet to come?

The massacre at My Lai may not have been known to the general public back home, but in country, we knew it had happened. Our battalion operated south of My Lai, and it didn't take long for that "shit part of the war" to hit the communication trapline of the grunt soldier. Almost all of us were shocked, and none of us thought it was right.

We discussed among ourselves how to deal with an improper order and decided that we would not do as we were told if faced with the same circumstance. However, we knew our leaders well by this time, and we sincerely believed no such unjust orders would ever be given. Lord knows, our experiences already had guaranteed we were gathering a lifetime of nightmares. We didn't need to add any more guilt and shame to our mental load.

I believe soldiers in combat come from good stock. They are skilled in their profession and destined to discharge their duties in an honorable way. I've seen my share of combat and have been in countless villages. We knew which ones were sympathetic to the VC and the Hanoi government. I never witnessed anything close to the atrocious maltreatment of civilians that transpired at My Lai. Even though some of my fellow grunts may have believed we had justification or provocation, no beatings were administered, no rapes occurred, and certainly, no executions took place during my time with the 26th Regiment, aka the Blue Spaders.

In our unit, everyone focused on keeping their cool and otherwise going about their business. Yes, a lot of yelling took place, and threats were made against many. If we encountered a weapons cache in a village hooch, we would burn it down, but not destroy the entire village. After all, a hooch was a thatched hut where families lived. There was no need to destroy all for the mistakes of a few.

We understood that most of the time, village inhabitants didn't have a choice but to provide aid to the enemy. We were not there to protect them twenty-four hours a day. These poor souls had to survive the best way they could. The VC were much more likely to kill the villagers than we were. These poor people simply wanted to feed their families and survive the war.

Deep down, the line grunt has a good soul. Even though we lost men in some of these villages, we always took the high road and did our best to win these people over. It was obvious to my command leadership that you cannot win the hearts and minds of the civilians if you burn down their villages and inflict unspeakable havoc on the population.

Unfortunately, the My Lai massacre gave many Americans the impression that all combat soldiers were "baby killers." Thus, another untrue characterization of an American soldier was born. All of us who returned from the Vietnam War have heard these kinds of terrible and untrue insults cast our way. It still pisses me off when I think about how the actions of a few can forever taint the reputations of so many.

Now that I got that off my chest, let me focus on some of the *good* things we did. There has not been a lot of ink about these positive expressions of humanity.

Many times, when we came across a village or hamlet, we would provide civic services. As the medic, I'd hold sick call and tend to the medical needs of the villagers, treating a variety of diseases and suturing wounds when required. I'd apply healing ointments and hand out candy to the kids. I came to realize that these poor civilians just wanted to live their lives in peace, free from harassment from anyone, including the Americans.

We visited quaint, indigenous Vietnamese hamlets where the inhabitants had never seen an American. Thankfully, on such missions of mercy, we had an interpreter who assured the villagers we were there to render assistance.

I quickly realized that sanitation was perhaps the biggest health impediment these humble but proud people faced. I dealt with a lot of infections and illnesses that could have been avoided if the villagers used soap and water on a regular basis. I was honored to remake life a little less difficult, if only for a short time.

I remember the kids most of all. Even though I thought their lives seemed hopeless and miserable, they were always upbeat and positive. I learned that no matter how difficult life is, you can be tolerant and look ahead to better times.

A sister looking out for her little brother in the bush.

Chapter 28

NDPs and APs

Vietnam required the development of more innovative tactics for nighttime fighting. These tactics were dictated by the fundamental combat differences from previous military conflicts. In retrospect, I believe these differences from previous wars were not at all understood by the powers who were making decisions in Washington, DC. Perhaps this lack of understanding eventually contributed to the reasons for our lack of "political solutions through military success" in Vietnam.

Night Defensive Perimeters (NDPs) proved essential for unit survival in an area of heavy enemy concentration. Employing this technique became standard operating procedure in the jungles of Vietnam and absolutely saved countless American lives and inflicted extensive damage on enemy forces.

From a military perspective, the Vietnam War required new and innovative techniques for engaging the enemy. Unlike WWI, WWII or the Korean Conflict, there was no defined front or conventional battle lines in Vietnam. It was a war of insurgency, and remote territory was frequently occupied by us for only a short period of time. When American forces identified a geographical area believed to contain NVA regiments, US soldiers were deployed to sweep the suspect locale by organizing search-and-destroy missions.

This new approach required troops to remain in an area for days or perhaps weeks at a time. As a result, the night defensive position tactic was developed to allow units to protect themselves at night. Eventually, we would leave the land we had briefly occupied only to return weeks later to reoccupy it once again. Although this was an interesting battle tactic, it eventually contributed to the long-term failure of winning the war.

Daytime search-and-destroy missions were offensive tactics designed to attack the enemy. Constructing a night defensive position was a defensive tactic that often invited the enemy to attack the perimeter while we protected it.

According to the Military Operations Reports of Battles, the 1st Infantry Division's operations illustrate many innovations used by infantry commanders in Vietnam. Well-planned night defensive positions enabled the infantry to take advantage of their new weapons with increased firepower, thereby making the foot soldier more effective. The night defensive position was also protected by artillery, gunships and tactical fighter support. Starlight scopes, trip flares, bells in the wire and Claymore mines also helped the perimeter guards stay alert and do their job.

The enemy always viewed these NDPs as a nuisance and a threat that must be eliminated. Consequently, nighttime attacks were frequent and usually devastating for the attackers. Because we were so well fortified by bunkers with sandbag roofs, the battle odds were clearly in our favor.

Let me put this approach into perspective. According to the description of a night enemy attack, written by Colonel Cavazos, near Loc Ninh in November 1967, one American was killed, and eight were wounded. That same night, 263 enemy soldiers were killed. These impressive statistics truly demonstrate the effectiveness of the NDP.

Another defensive tactic to protect the NDP was the listening post (LP) and ambush patrols (AP). Both involved stealth and surprise. Their goal was to intercept the enemy before they reached the NDP and alert the NDP to any enemy activity. Soldiers assigned to these defensive missions needed to stay alert and ready for action. Everyone's life depended on this.

Ambush patrols were chaotic and very tough duty. Most often, the patrol was made up of one squad. As a medic, I pulled three times as many night-ambush patrols as the regular infantry. The reason for this can be determined by using simple math. There are three squads in a platoon but only one medic. Whenever a ten-man squad went on a patrol, including night patrols, the medic went along. I called myself the "Eleventh Man!"

By now, you must wonder why I, the medic, know so much about these standard infantry tactics. It's because of my continuously evolving "on-the-job training" and my never-ending quest for making sure I survived. I'm very observant and, by necessity, participated in more patrols than anyone else in the platoon. In addition to countless daytime patrols, I pulled around sixty night-ambush patrols during my tour in Vietnam.

One time, even though I was a medic, I was asked to write a report on the effectiveness of night patrols based on my personal experiences. I was told my report was sent to division headquarters to determine if my insights would benefit others.

I pulled three times as many APs as the regular riflemen and never let my cohorts forget it. Our job was to break up any enemy forces heading toward the NDP. APs were an extremely stressful exercise because there were only eleven of us to execute the ambush, and it was not uncommon for us to piss off an enemy force ten times our size.

When we blew the ambush and surprised the enemy, we waited for the initial firing to slow down and then retreated to the safety of the perimeter. Setting off an ambush and surprising a hostile force was a thrilling experience that always resulted in an immense adrenaline rush. Sometimes when one of our team was wounded, we would hunker down and fight it out.

A night extraction of a non-mobile casualty was next to impossible in jungle terrain. These occasions produced long, sleepless, nerve-wracking nights. But I survived and lived to treat the injured for at least one more day.

I was involved in more firefights at night, but we suffered relatively few causalities. I suspect this is due in part to the fact it was dark, we were well concealed, and we were the ones who surprised the enemy. During the day, we were the ones being surprised and ambushed by the enemy. They knew our location and had the advantage in an attack. I treated more soldiers during the daylight hours.

Taking a break to get our bearings on another long day of search and destroy patrols.

Chapter 29

Race Relations in a Combat Unit

When I arrived at my unit, I was the FNG replacing a well-seasoned medic who happened to be black. It didn't take me long to realize that half of the unit was black, and as a reflection of the times, there was a degree of suspicion about this white boy medic. Being an FNG was tough enough, but replacing a combat-tested black medic put additional pressure on me. But here I was, the new grunt "doc." I needed to figure out my role and how to handle myself. I knew I would need to earn the respect of my combat brothers, regardless of their ethnicity.

Being from Minnesota, I hadn't met many black guys. My basic training unit included just a few from a National Guard unit in Alabama. Otherwise, the rest were all white guys. Several told me they had to give up their membership in the KKK because the military makes you swear allegiance to the US Constitution, and KKK memberships are prohibited. From that perspective, basic training provided me with a good education about the many social differences and mindsets of people from different parts of the country. Most of us were draftees and reflected the cultural makeup of America.

I liked the black guys I met in basic training. Most of my drill cadre were black. I didn't think much about our color differences. While I didn't have any preconceived notions, I certainly could sense some tension between the white and black soldiers, particularly if they were from the south.

When I joined my unit in Vietnam, I estimated half of Company A was black. The Army did not discuss such things, so I didn't think too much about the reason for this anomaly until I started writing this book. It didn't take me long to discover that the Vietnam War had the highest proportion of blacks ever to serve in an American war.

I also learned that "African Americans often did supply a disproportionate number of combat troops, a high percentage of whom had voluntarily enlisted. Although they made up less than 10 percent of American men in arms and about 13 percent of the US population between 1961 and 1966, they accounted for almost 20 percent of all combat-related deaths in Vietnam during that period. In 1965 alone, African Americans represented almost one-fourth of the Army's killed in action. In 1968 African Americans, who made up roughly 12 percent of Army and Marine total strengths, frequently contributed half the men in front-line combat units, especially in rifle squads and fire teams."[1]

There didn't seem to be much racial tension in my company. I gathered from personal experience and some limited research on this subject that race was rarely an issue in combat units because we all shared the same duties and watched out for each other. We equally shared the same risk, and we all took orders from each other regardless of skin color. Racial strife was more evident in the rear areas and on domestic military installations, particularly after the assassination of Dr. Martin Luther King, Jr. His tragic assassination on April 4, 1968, was truly a shot heard around the world because it didn't take long for this tragic news to reach our unit in Vietnam.

The details of King's death reached us in the field the next day when the re-supply chopper brought ammo, food, mail and news from the "world," as we called it. As if things weren't tough enough, the news made us feel even more stress and tension. The word of Dr. King's murder by a white guy spread rapidly, and soldiers gathered in small groups sorted by skin color to talk about it. I believed Dr. King was a good man and was someone very special to the black soldiers.

---

1   From *The Oxford Companion to American Military History.*

I eventually discovered how important the truths that he expressed would become to all citizens. I knew that Dr. King sought equality through peace and social justice. He died because of his beliefs as he preached peace and hope. He clearly wanted to make America a better place for every citizen. I thought about his ideology and realized we were in a combat zone fighting for these same principles for the South Vietnamese people.

I think there would have been a lot more unrest in the field but for the quality of our small unit Army leaders. Our officers and non-com sergeants were sensitive to the needs of all of us. To a man, we trusted them. During this time of home-front racial disruption, our leaders (both black and white) kept everything cool. There were genuine expressions of heartfelt sadness and shock. To me, Dr. King's assassination and Bobby Kennedy's murder a few months later caused us to wonder, "What in the hell is happening in our country back home?" *Get it together, people! If we can get along in a war zone, why can't you just love one another and care for your neighbor?*

But that was 1968, and things in the United States were going to get much worse before they got better, as we all know.

Like everyone in the unit, I had to earn every man's confidence by doing my job to the best of my ability. Soon enough, I proved my value and achieved "trust status" when I treated my first casualty. He happened to be a white guy who had received a few minor cuts and fragment injuries from a not-so-effective booby trap. He was lucky, and so was I. But he was a causality just the same. He got a Purple Heart, and I started off on my on-the-job training as a physical fixer upper.

I soon discovered I was still a bit suspect to some of the black soldiers, even though we all bleed the same color. Most of them were raised in the south and grew up with a different attitude than I did having been raised in Minnesota. It still seems a little odd, but the black troops wondered if I would render aid to them the same way I did to the white soldiers. *Crazy, huh?* Perhaps this concern reflected their upbringing and how the principles of segregation got in the way of dealing with trauma in their hometowns.

Wow, this kind of thinking was strange to me and quite concerning. Societal perceptions and combat perceptions came to a head in the least likely of all places, a war zone in Vietnam.

In our unit, and I expect in all things military, people referred to each other by our last names. Sometimes, people earned a nickname or were given one by the group if their last name was difficult to pronounce or remember. Apparently, Strusinski was a hard name for some people to pronounce, particularly if they were from the south and not routinely exposed to people of Polish descent. Most of my fellow soldiers referred to me as "Pollack" or "Doc," depending on the amount of intended endearment.

I remember the time I earned a new nickname. It was bestowed immediately after I treated my first black casualty. We were on a patrol, and the point man, who happened to be black, was wounded by grenade fragments. Fortunately, it was an unlucky toss by the would-be assassin. The grenade hit a tree and bounced off, landing about fifteen feet away from the point man. The grenade exploded, but the guy's wounds were relatively minor, and the enemy sniper was eliminated.

Per my routine, I ran toward the yell for the medic. I treated his wounds and determined that he was going to survive. I then called in a dust-off for evacuation to the field hospital.

The black soldiers on patrol that day took notice of my actions. They seemed a bit surprised as I rushed forward to the black soldier and provided aid the same way I did for the wounded white soldier. While I didn't think anything of it, they sure did.

As an expression of their appreciation, and I think in response to my unbiased attitude, the black guys began to call me "Soullock" instead of "Pollack!" Without realizing it, I had passed their racial test and was accepted. I've reflected on that incident over the years and always thought such acceptance was pretty darn special.

Now I was a fully accepted member of the platoon, bestowed with the honor and trust that medics were typically afforded. My elevated status in life would later prove to be especially useful. One night, while we were relaxing at our base camp, I was beckoned by several black soldiers who pleaded with me to resolve a major dispute. Several men had been playing high stakes poker to pass the time in base camp. Alcohol, cards, money and guns always make for an interesting evening of participatory entertainment. On this particular occasion, however, the entertainment was interspersed with terror.

The platoon sergeant had been enjoying the friendly game but then his good fortune and happy disposition changed to bad luck and financial loss. He became a bit upset, which made the others a little uneasy. Well, maybe a *lot* uneasy! As was the custom, the loser, along with the other poker players and observers, was quite drunk. Soon enough, his mood soured because he believed some of the big winners were cheating. He became very angry, then tipped over the poker table, threatened violence and headed straight to his bunk.

His intentions soon became obvious. He retrieved his M-15 carbine and loaded a magazine. The M-15 carbine is a short version of an M-16 rifle and only issued to senior sergeants and officers. The angry staff sergeant was now fully prepared to administer his brand of jungle combat justice.

Everyone in the tent was highly skilled at recognizing danger when they saw it. The rapidly sobering soldiers acted as one and, like all prudent men, ran out of the tent and headed for cover, me included. From the bunker adjacent to the tent, the men hurriedly exchanged ideas on what to do about this drunk and unhappy sergeant with a loaded M-15.

A quick plan was hatched. It was simple enough in concept but more difficult in execution. The plan required someone to disarm the angry sergeant.

As it so often went in times of peril and distress, the men look to the medic for guidance and action. They concluded that I should be the one to calm the situation and resolve the dispute. That line of reasoning may have made sense to the others, but it made very little sense to me.

As soon as I objected to this ill-conceived plan, the black guys insisted that "Soullock" was the only person who could unruffle the upset sergeant and calmly talk him into surrendering his loaded rifle. In other words, they didn't think he would shoot *me*.

The expression "didn't think he would shoot me" was not the level of confidence of success that I was hoping to hear.

I mumbled something like, "Why me, oh Lord, why me?"

The angry sergeant was from Hell's Kitchen in New York and was one tough dude. In contrast, I was a mild-mannered white boy from Minnesota. As in combat, my adrenaline started to flow, and I became focused on the dangerous task ahead. If I was going to be the one to settle this matter, I had to calm myself down, engage my brain and find my nerve.

I finally agreed to the plan and set out to execute the plan. As I re-entered the hooch, I was thinking, *How in the hell are they going to explain to my mother the circumstances surrounding my untimely death?*

Summoning all the courage I could muster, which wasn't much, I calmly walked up to the malcontent and blocked his pathway to the others. He stopped in his tracks and in a quivering voice said, "Get out of the way, Doc!"

In a firm, unwavering voice, I shouted, "Sergeant, you are not going to kill any friendlies tonight. Now give me that goddamn rifle and go to bed!" This was not exactly the way I had intended to calm him down.

We stood there for a few seconds staring at each other. *Was he sizing me up? Does it hurt when you get shot?* His breathing was rapid, and he was sweating profusely. These were classic symptoms of anger, stress and high anxiety—not good signs for me and could directly impact my longevity.

Then, without saying a word, he handed me the gun, did an about-face and went to bed. Situation resolved, back to normal.

None of us could believe it, but we were elated at the outcome. Just for comfort, I slept with his rifle all night in the event he awoke and reconsidered his actions.

In the morning, he didn't remember much about the night before, or so he said. I guess medics *do* have some influence over combat soldiers.

When I think about the difficult times my unit encountered back then, I'm pleased with how we responded to crises and solved problems no matter how tough they were. I'm grateful to have known these men and to have survived my tour. There was an honest comfort in knowing that any of us would lay down his life for another regardless of his race. We didn't talk about it because we didn't have to.

I think that men who engage in combat don't have time to philosophize about how they feel. In the face of danger and hurt, they instinctively act. I wish the public would respect each other the same way our interracial band of brothers did in Vietnam. In our hearts, we trusted each other to do the right thing. If war can foster cooperation and trust, surely people in peace can do the same. People must learn to get along.

I need to add a qualification to this discussion. My observations are solely based on personal experiences in 1967 and 1968. Although civil unrest and racial tension were on the rise in the US in 1968, we didn't hear much about it except for the assassination of Martin Luther King. Hell, we hardly ever got *any* news on what was happening back home unless such information was in a letter someone received. Usually, the contents of the correspondence from family and friends was kept light and nonpolitical.

While we didn't sit around the old campfire, we did sit around the bunkers and shoot the shit about our day's activities. I don't recall much conversation about stateside politics and social change. We spent time engaged in more practical conversations about battles, weapons, women and whiskey!

I am sure the soldiers who came to Vietnam after my tour ended in August of 1968 were more aware of the unrest in the States. I have since learned that soldiers, in general, became more socially dysfunctional and suffered more unease over civil rights issues. Eventually, drugs crept in and created a new havoc. I do believe, however, that the level of tension was not as great in combat units as it was among support personnel. I was very surprised at the significant amount of dissent over civil rights and the war when I rotated home in late 1968.

Sadly, many students turned their anger towards the soldiers who were fighting for them and who merely did what they were asked to do. This was not a good time for returning veterans, myself included. It was bullshit back then, and the mental pain made all of us feel less than friendly toward the hippies and draft dodgers.

Most Vietnam veterans returning to civilian life and college campuses hated the protestors and the anti-government movement. For most of us, these wounds will never heal. As Bob Dylan wrote, "The Times, They Are A-Changin!"

Chapter 30

Out of the Field and Back at Headquarters

The month of May was relatively calm. By now, the Viet Cong and NVA were back in Cambodia and Laos, where they were licking their wounds and rebuilding their combat units. The TET Offensive was not good for them, and they suffered so many casualties they needed to rebuild their army. We encountered a few snipers and engaged in some minor firefights but had no major battles. I spent most of my time dealing with soldiers' cuts, scrapes, snake bites, jungle rot and a multiplicity of infections, including venereal diseases.

By June, I was spending more time at headquarters company (HHC) and the Battalion Aid Station. I pulled a few more civic action patrols. Even though Military Assistance Command Vietnam (MACV) instructed us to increase our efforts to win the hearts and minds of the local civilian population, I believed in our mission to help those civilians who were caught in the misfortunes of war. At least we could feel good about helping people—Lord knows we destroyed the lives of many of them.

The local population had an uncertain future, and hardships would remain the norm for years to come. Frequently, our efforts were about trying to make a desperate situation more hopeful. We continued to try to be good neighbors in this war zone by executing humanitarian missions, but even the optimists among us were becoming despondent.

At the end of June, I was officially rotated out of the field and assigned to duty at the Battalion Aide station in Quan Loi, our base camp. It was my tenth month in country. I understood the need for my longer tenure on the line because my battalion had suffered a lot of casualties, including the loss of several medics.

During this phase of the war, replacement soldiers were in short supply. Our combat company could only muster ninety to a hundred men on a good day. Of course, we could always access an unlimited supply of bullets, grenades, C-rations and cigarettes.

A typical Army infantry company has one hundred fifty men. As the draft buildup increased in 1968, plenty of soldiers eventually arrived to fill the ranks, thus making my rotation out of the field possible. It was probably poor planning on the part of the high command because they sent too many medics to hospitals in Germany and Italy. *Bastards*!

Working back at the battalion aid station was great because I got to help the battalion physician with more complicated, non-battle related injuries. I assisted in minor surgical procedures and had an ever-increasing opportunity to engage in social conversations that went beyond "fuck the brass and all of their chicken shit ideas." It was easier duty and much safer. I was relishing more free time, and I made the best of it. My spare time was spent writing letters, playing cards and reading instead of cleaning weapons and playing stretch with our bayonets.

Back in the rear, I finally lived in a tent with screen sides and a wooden floor. I had an Army-issued bed, not a cot, complete with a mattress, clean sheets and a pillow. I could sleep in my underwear, but I always kept my boots and M-16 handy in case of attack. Finally, I was living the good life. Compared to the field, it was pure luxury that included three hot meals and a hot shower every day. Many nights were spent at the enlisted men's club, where we swapped stories and enjoyed past bravado over beers and whiskey. We deeply appreciated the occasional Philippine floor shows with sweet girls singing the latest American rock music.

The author is working on a tan and writing a letter home.

The daily routine included treating those on sick call and sending re-supplies to the medics in the field. Since the aide station needed to be staffed twenty-four hours a day, I pulled overnight duty every fifth night. There was not much activity unless the sporadic bar fight combatants required sutures or dressings. Best of all, I was nearing the date of my separation (DEROS) from Vietnam, and my new assignment meant I would only go back into combat if we lost other medics in the battalion, or if another TET-like enemy surge erupted. This new job was much better duty than my previous field medic work.

Being a rear echelon medic did not mean I was immune from anguish or despair. The war continued, and firefights took their toll on the troops. My time in Vietnam was not quite over. There was more sadness for me to endure.

I still have great sorrow over a situation that occurred in July just a few weeks before I left Vietnam. I was in the aid station monitoring the command radio as standard operating procedure dictated. If something happened in the bush, we could hear the command traffic and determine if re-supplies or support personal were needed.

On this sunny day, my old unit, Company A, was ambushed while on a search-and-destroy patrol along the Song Be River. They took many casualties, and two guys were killed. I had been a proud member of that company for the previous ten months and knew most of these men.

As the firefight increased in intensity, several Cobra gunships and Air Force fighter jets were dispatched to help relieve the battered company. The battle was tough enough, but the situation was about to get much worse.

Our battalion commander, who carried the rank of Lt. Colonel, was circling overhead in a light observation helicopter (LOH) observing the action and giving directions to the troops on the ground. He could see the enemy consolidating forces and merging on Company A's position. The colonel alerted the captain in charge of Company A of this activity and rearranged the remaining ground forces into a better defensive position.

Soon enough, air support arrived on station and began executing strafing runs, firing into the now sizable enemy force. The situation worsened as the enemy started throwing smoke grenades that were the same color as those thrown by Company A. The enemy knew that the colored smoke was a common location identifier to the gunships and fighters for depositing their ordnance. Deploying the same color smoke confused the air support teams.

This was an intentional enemy technique they hoped would spare their forces from injury. Predictably, one of the F-4 Phantom jets providing overhead fire support mistakenly dropped two bombs on Company A's position. Several friendlies were killed, and many others wounded. While being exposed to friendly fire was not uncommon, in this case, it was devastating.

The Colonel had nothing but harsh words for the F-4 pilot that day. I could tell the pilot was devastated. He asked to make another bombing run on the correct trajectory, but the Colonel told him to "get the hell out of the area—I'll deal with you later."

This was but one more lesson of war. Friendly fire happens, and bombs are indiscriminate. We all must understand the unintentional consequences of war and be prepared to live forever with the aftermath.

Among the fatalities were the first sergeant and a medic. The company desperately needed more support troops, a medic and ammo, and they needed it fast. The end of the battle was nowhere in sight.

The call for a medic and more medical supplies came across the Battalion Aid Station radio. I began to assemble the necessary supplies and muster my nerves for action. I felt the adrenaline start to flow as I grabbed my aid bag. I was not happy because my tour was almost over, and the very last thing I wanted to do was get back into the shit.

While I was organizing my thoughts and supplies, a medic with lower rank volunteered to bring the supplies and join the fight instead of me. He knew I only had a few weeks left in country, and he had a few months to go. I was very relieved and gratefully accepted his generous offer. He was a good man and I admired his courage. He was a religious man and told me God would protect him.

I took the needed medical supplies to a waiting slick for the short helicopter trip to the beleaguered company while my pal retrieved his aid bag. I will forever remember the look of confidence on his face as he boarded the rescue chopper and bravely headed toward the after-carnage of the firefight.

Regrettably, that young medic, who had a wife and child back home, was killed when the resupply chopper was shot down, heading into the landing zone. Like many other soldiers who died in Vietnam, his child would grow up not knowing his father was a man of great conscience and courage. That incident sent a chill over me as I realized once again it could have been me. The guilt began immediately, and the question, "Why not me, Lord?" has stayed with me to this day.

Learning to live with survivor's guilt is very difficult. But we do learn to live with it because we must. Like many other regrets from

Vietnam, I have rationalized that decision and stored the entire incident away in my mind. I retrieve that story when I need it to educate others about the lifelong after-effects of war on soldiers.

Chapter 31

Government Decision Making

During my tenure in a combat company, I developed a curiosity about government decision-making. My thinking evolved while in the field because we had many hours to contemplate complex subjects. A guy can only spend so much time writing letters home. In any event, I was dismayed at a couple of high-level decisions that prompted me to figure out how I could get involved with government after the Army. I believed my experience in combat would help me make better decisions and benefit more people than the decisions made by our political leaders. After all, I was now a combat veteran, and I was used to solving problems.

An example of the government's decision-making issue is the inability of the Paris Peace Accord negotiators to agree on the type and shape of the table around which to meet. It took months to agree on using a round table so no one would have a perceived advantage. I could have made that decision in a few minutes. From a soldier's perspective, that discussion was trivial and overly prolonged. In this war, countless combatants could die waiting for the treaty discussions to begin, let alone conclude. *Who's in charge of making these decisions? What a bunch of crap!*

Another example of poor decision-making was an incident involving North Korea. In January 1968, our unit was pulled from the field and assembled at the airport in Quan Loi. We sat there all night waiting to be loaded onto planes for some undisclosed destination. In the morning, we received orders to stand down. We were subsequently transported by helicopter back into the bush.

I asked the First Sergeant what that escapade was about? To my surprise, he said, "A navy ship called the Pueblo was captured by North Korea." He went on to explain, "We were recalled from the field along with several other combat units of the First Infantry Division to prepare to invade North Korea and get our ship back." *Wow. Someone decided to take a fully seasoned combat Division out of the Vietnam War to start a new war in North Korea?*

I remember discussing my frustration with my buddies. We all wondered, "Who was the idiot who was supposed to making these decisions?" The group concluded that any one of us could do better.

A few weeks later, I went to Japan for some R&R. While there, I looked up a friend from the days when I spent my summers traveling with a carnival to make money for school. My friend was in the Air Force, so we connected over dinner and a lot of cocktails. As I recall, the proportion of intelligent conversation was related to the amount of alcohol we consumed. We were both pretty smart talkers that night.

I told him about our troops' reactions to the capture of the Pueblo and our "almost invasion" battleplan. He said, "Let me tell you my story about the same incident." As a flight controller in the Air Force, he was in the command tower at the airport the day the Pueblo was captured. His recollection of that event left nothing to speculation.

The USS Pueblo, he told me, was a spy ship. The air force had provided a couple of fighters and a bomber to provide air cover because the Pueblo was sailing in international waters. To the apparent surprise of the commander of the Pueblo, several gunboats came out of the North Korean harbor and attacked the ship, demanding its surrender.

This is where the story gets even more intriguing. Evidently, the planes providing air cover were all armed with tactical nuclear weapons and had no conventional bombs that could be used against aggressors. Consequently, all aircraft were ordered to immediately return to Japan so they could be rearmed with conventional bombs. By the time these rearmed fighters reunited over the Pueblo, the ship was already docked in the North Korean harbor. As a result, the decision was made to stand down, so no bombs were dropped.

Wow. Only tactical nuclear weapons? I thought. *No conventional bombs? Who made that decision?* To me, it seemed unconscionable to have combat aircraft flying dangerous missions with only nuclear weapons in their arsenal.

No doubt, a couple of high-explosive bombs dropped on a North Korean gunboat would have ended this ordeal in our favor. But that was not the case.

Who was making these decisions? I wondered. *Tactical nuclear weapons in fighter jets? Sending my unit of the Army to invade North Korea? Difficulty agreeing on the shape of the peace negotiations table?* It was easy for my humble brain and ego to conclude that even I could make dumb-ass decisions like these—and maybe my decisions would be better.

From an infantry perspective, we all believed we were geniuses. It was abundantly clear to most ground pounders that there needed to be a genius of our caliber—or at a minimum, a soldier of average intelligence—involved in the chain of decision-making. We needed more focus and better solutions to the policy doctrines that our country was pursuing.

At this point, I knew the impact of any decision could really hurt. The result of my musings about such weighty matters eventually helped me identify the steps I needed to take after I left the Army. I wanted to apply the lessons I had learned in combat to the task of creating a more tranquil nation—a nation that could continue to provide a better life for all citizens regardless of race or religious beliefs. I wanted all of us to become successful and enjoy the rewards earned from exercising good judgment and personal responsibility.

This was my epiphany, and I now had a plan. *When I get out of the Army I will go back to college and get a degree in political science. Upon graduating, I will engage in politics and set about making change. I believed I can be a force for better decision-making within the government structure and on behalf of all citizens.*

And that is what I did. My military experiences truly served as the catalyst for my personal career plan of action. Maybe this was all worth it, after all!

Chapter 32

Going Home and Personal Reflections

Eventually, all good things must come to an end. On August 8, 1968, I left Quan Loi and began my long journey back home. On the uneventful helicopter ride to the Bien Hoa airport, I kept singing the words from a song made famous by the Animals, "We gotta get out of this place, if it's last thing we ever do."

A day later, I boarded a TWA jet that would return me to my family and hopefully to a life of peace. I was very excited to be leaving Vietnam and didn't spend much time saying farewell to my brothers. They were all happy for me, of course, but I was sad for them. I knew the daily grind of search-and-destroy patrols would continue. I was also very sad to discover later that several of my pals were killed after I left country.

Could I have saved any of them if I were on patrol and at their side? Probably not, as I am sure my replacement medic did a fine job. Never look back, or so they say, because heartache is but a gunshot away.

I was looking forward to seeing my family and enjoying a thirty-day leave. Because my tour of duty in Vietnam occurred during leap year, I was concerned about getting killed on day 366. Fortunately, my luck held. I was one happy man as I climbed aboard that flight to return home. We called it "the freedom bird."

Upon takeoff, the planeload of returnees erupted in applause, happy to leave the trauma and sorrow behind. We loudly sang along with the music that had greeted us upon take off. Our transport pilot clearly wanted to make us comfortable. He set the proper mood for take-off by loudly playing the same song I had been singing, "We Gotta Get Out of This Place."

We shed tears of joy as we belted out that tune. In truth, most of us were unable to leave our bad memories behind and still carried them. The cabin attendants were as beautiful as angels. They served fresh fruit and milk. *What a treat!* These ladies charmed us with warm smiles and an occasional embrace, all of which were appreciated. It was the best plane ride of my life.

The flight provided a great opportunity to reflect upon my tour of duty and the things I had learned. The full range of my Army medical experiences included treating snake bites, scorpion stings, scrapes, scratches, puncture wounds, dysentery, fire ant bites, hepatitis, infections from leeches and centipedes, jungle rot, broken bones, toothaches, gunshot wounds, shrapnel wounds, punji stick wounds, traumatic stress syndrome, land mine injuries and burns. I had sutured wounds, gave mouth to mouth resuscitation, administered morphine and applied splints. I had dealt with attempted suicides and treated self-inflicted wounds. Too often, I had acted as a counselor when personalities clashed, when alcohol-induced disagreements surfaced or when one of the guys got a "Dear John" letter.

I had also tended to an assortment of maladies afflicting Vietnamese villagers while I was engaged in Civic Action Patrols. It had been quite a year, to say the least. Now, my thoughts turned to how to apply these skills in a meaningful way as I move onto the next phase of my life. It didn't take me long to realize that civilians are not routinely exposed to the same trauma as combat soldiers.

My "freedom bird" touched down at Oakland Air Force Base some twenty-four hours after we left Vietnam. As I disembarked, I felt a lump in my throat. Tears of joy erupted from my eyes. After kissing the ground, I boarded a bus that took us to our military processing center.

As we departed the airport, we were greeted by a crowd of protestors who shouted insults and threw eggs and other garbage at our bus. They carried signs with disparaging comments like "baby killer" and "shame on you" on them. They shouted insults and spit and kicked the bus, attempting to disrupt our excursion into friendly territory. *What a homecoming.* We were all stunned and regretted not having our combat gear so we could extend a "welcome home greeting to these bastards" in *our own* highly skilled way.

I was dumbfounded by all the protestors. We were shocked to witness a demonstration directed against *us*, of all people. Most of us had no sympathy for their cause and felt betrayed by their behavior.

We angrily asked the driver to pull over so we could "properly address" the situation, but the young private wisely continued driving us to the separation facility. The incident was just the first of many we would endure. Clearly, reconciliation was going to take years to achieve. Maybe it would never happen. Maybe reconciliation wouldn't make a difference anyway. This discussion would continue for decades.

The bus eventually made its way to the assembly facility, where we were treated to steak and eggs, potatoes and lots of toast dripping with butter. The unlimited supply of fresh milk was refreshing. We ate until we could eat no more. We also exchanged countless war stories and expressed concern about being back in the good old USA. So far, it didn't seem much like the country we had left a year earlier.

Very soon, I had my leave orders and some travel money, so it was time to begin the final leg of my journey home. The Army provided me with one more ride to the Los Angeles airport for a non-stop flight to St. Paul. I don't remember any protester incidents at the airport. That was good because I don't think my mindset would have allowed me to act responsibly if I had come face-to-face with any protesters.

My mom and dad were waiting at the gate, and I was overwhelmed with emotion as I dashed into their loving arms. I'll always cherish that first welcome home hug from Mom. It makes me cry even now just to think about it.

The shock of being home hit me at last, and adrenaline started pumping. But this time it felt different. It wasn't brought on by fear, but by joy. I knew I was a changed man. From war zone to home had only taken twenty-four hours, which is not enough time to adjust to the conversations of civilian life. You'd think the military would understand that a smooth transition can't be completed in such a short period of time.

For most of us, it would take years to cope with the ordeal of coming home and dealing with the complexities of being in an English-speaking society that wasn't ready to accept us.

Fortunately, my thirty-day leave would give me time to relax and contemplate life. I planned on visiting my old friends on the carnival midway. That had been a great, nomadic life that had allowed me to develop many skills, including how to read people and to appreciate the importance of customer service. These skills had easily transferred to my military job as a medic.

It had been quite a year. I went into the Army a novice and was honorably discharged a veteran. I was transformed from a teenager who knew little about life to a young man who now had a lifetime of memories and stories, some good and others I'd rather forget but can't.

In war, every day brought more experiences and new challenges. I don't remember ever being bored. I learned to make some very tough decisions and then live with the consequences. I lived by the credo that "when your time is up, your life will end." You can't avoid it, but you can prepare for it. That is why there are no atheists in the infantry.

My uncertainty about life after the Vietnam War caused me to touch all the spiritual bases. When the time arose to surrender my fate to a power higher than the first sergeant, I sought comfort from God, Buddha, Allah, the Dalai Lama, the sun, the trees and even the rocks.

Unfortunately, this approach to prayer made it difficult to figure out which spiritual entity was contributing to my survival. Certainly, one of them had to be the Supreme Deity—perhaps all of them were—because I made it home. On the other hand, I sometimes wondered,

Were we spared by luck, fate or Divine intervention? If Divine intervention had spared us, then why were some religious men killed or wounded, and the rest of us were not?

My gut tells me it was good luck. After all, my mother was Irish, and she strongly believed in the value of a four-leaf clover and the value of respecting leprechauns. I must have genetically inherited her good fortune.

In war, we grunts needed to have the mindset of "When your number's up, it's up. Nothing you can do about it." Perhaps that blind trust in absorbing life as it came our way, combined with the power of positive thinking, enabled all soldiers to keep doing what needed to be done. None of us wanted to get a Purple Heart because a lot of them were awarded posthumously.

In general, the Army gave medals to soldiers who did their job. In some cases, they were awarded for valor because a superior officer had witnessed an action by someone who, in his estimation, performed above the normal call of duty. It was an honor to receive such recognition, but as all recipients will attest, they seldom thought they had done anything extraordinary.

I received three Bronze Stars for valor during my tour in Vietnam. I'll spare the details, but from my perspective, I had done nothing that any other soldier in a similar situation wouldn't have done.

The real heroes were the ones who gave their lives for their combat brothers and their country. I was just the guy trying to save them. I was the medic, and that was my job. Sometimes the wounded made it out alive, and I was happy for them. In those cases, I was merely an instrument of sanity and hope in a world of chaos and hurt.

The award I'm most proud of is my Combat Medical Badge (CMB). Soldiers in the infantry earn the Combat Infantry Badge, which demonstrates they honorably served in combat. The CMB recognizes my service with a combat infantry unit. It represents to me all the hardships we had to overcome, all the enemies we had to battle, and all the anxiety we had to endure. It also testifies that I truly cared about my wounded brothers and always did the best I could under very difficult situations.

Other medals I earned were the Army Commendation medal for overall meritorious achievement and leadership skills, and the Good Conduct medal for not misbehaving and maintaining mission readiness.

I was also awarded the Army Air medal for making more than twenty-five combat air assaults by helicopter. I was surprised by that one because I wasn't keeping count.

My Blue Spader unit received several awards from the South Vietnamese government for distinction under combat. We all received the Vietnamese service medal.

In the final analysis, I am proud of my medals because they reflect my commitment to my brothers while at the same time demonstrating my failure to get a hospital job in Germany! I am no one special, but I did survive, and I beat the odds. *Lucky me!*

Chapter 33

Stateside Duty and the Path to an Honorable Discharge

After my leave, I was ordered to report to Fort Carson, Colorado. I was assigned to the 5th Infantry Division, which was a mechanized unit. Wearing the red diamond patch, this capable fighting unit was scheduled to go to Vietnam in seven months. That was fine with me because it would be one month after I was discharged from the Army, and even the federal government can't send civilians to war.

Fort Carson was pleasant, and the duty was easy. I bought a 1956 Oldsmobile from a soldier who was getting out and used it tour Colorado on weekends. As was the custom for base cars, I sold my dependable steed to another returning Vietnam vet when I left the Army.

The only tense time I remember at Fort Carson was during the first anniversary of the assassination of Dr. Martin Luther King, Jr. Leaders in Washington were rightfully worried about massive riots throughout the country in protest of King's murder. Fearing the inability of local officials to adequately deal with these anticipated riots, our division was put on alert. Should the need arise, our unit was supposed to move into Washington, DC, to restore order. Thankfully, nothing happened—I couldn't have taken up arms against my fellow citizens.

We spent our time keeping our medical tracks and ambulances in top-notch condition. We'd head to the motor pool after breakfast, sit inside the tracks and play cards. Don't get me wrong, we got our work done, but we did have time to rediscover the evils of poker.

Occasionally, we had to go on field exercises and simulate war games. Many of us were Vietnam veterans, so we didn't need much simulation. But practice we did, because we were still soldiering and did what we were told.

One day, during field exercises in February, a Jeep rolled over, and the driver was pinned beneath with a broken back. I was the senior medic on duty and surrounded by new folks. I thought, *Here we go again! More on-the-job training.* All eyes were on me. Some of the guys panicked, but I did not. It was just another situation where I had to take charge and address the problem.

This guy was hurt quite badly and needed immediate evacuation. A track or ambulance ride to the hospital was out of the question, so I called for dust-off, which would make the transport ride smoother and quicker.

It was hard to believe that I was facing a Jeep accident injury after all the firefights I'd been through. Nevertheless, it was a nerve-wracking experience because I knew one slight screw-up could kill him or, at minimum, cripple the guy for life. We lifted the Jeep and began treating his injuries. With great caution, I stabilized his back and neck. The others helped strap him to a backboard.

The dust-off soon arrived, and I tossed a smoke grenade to mark where I wanted the chopper to land. I talked the pilot to the ground, and we loaded our stateside casualty onto the chopper. As in Vietnam, I felt great relief when we got him on the transport without further mishap. The flight from the mountain to the emergency room only took ten minutes. I was later told we did an excellent job saving this man's life. In typical Army fashion, I was not given any further information, so I never learned if he had suffered a permanent disability.

My final military goal was to keep it simple and avoid hassles. Fortunately, this period passed quickly. On March 9, 1969, I received my Honorable Discharge and took a train ride home. Later that fall, I returned to Mankato State College to continue the education that had been interrupted in 1966 by the war. At least the US Government, through the GI Bill, was going to pay for my tuition.

Chapter 34

Political Lessons Learned and My Shift in Thinking

George Santayana, a noted philosopher, essayist, poet and novelist, wrote, "Those who do not remember the past are condemned to repeat it." I agree with his sentiment. I believe the takeaways from the Vietnam experience should prohibit the nation from entering new wars unless the objective is clear from both a military and political perspective.

The history surrounding the Vietnam War reminds us that millions of lives were forever affected by a few political leaders who relied on flawed intelligence and misapplied the sacred principals of service to God and Country. I sincerely hope we can learn from this experience and apply a new, higher standard before committing soldiers to die in future wars.

Many of us cannot escape thinking about our experiences. Consequently, politicians must be required to comprehend and think about the sacrifices we made and consider the impact their "political" decisions have on people's lives. Every American must insist our country's leaders learn from the past and resolve never to allow the political misjudgments that occurred during the Vietnam War to occur in the future. From my perspective, directing soldiers to fight and die in an unwinnable war was not only a regrettable mistake but must also be recognized as a profoundly teachable moment in our nation's history.

I've had more than five decades to reflect upon life in a war zone and a society in turmoil. I ponder some aspect of my time in the Vietnam War every day. Perhaps I'm just seeking closure or a better understanding of the influence those experiences had on the rest of my life. After all, it is easy to remember the tough times because there didn't seem to be that many good times. To me, the Vietnam War is a composite of raw occurrences that deserve reflection by those who served, those who protested, and those who must make political decisions based on the lessons from that time.

My thoughts are not just about false perceptions and flawed political leaders, but even more about truth and good public policy development. When old men send young men to die, it is incumbent upon them to explain why. I am not necessarily talking about generals directing soldiers into combat, although I would hope they too would have a good reason for doing so. Generals, however, are told what to do by presidents and Washington politicians who have supposedly exercised good judgment in developing policies of historical consequence.

If we want to preserve our form of democratic government and truly assure "liberty for all," we must learn from the combat heartache and social civil disruption of the 1960s and 70s.

I wrote one hundred and sixty letters to my parents, and many others to family members and friends. My mother kept all my letters and gave them to me just before she died. It took decades before I was emotionally prepared to read them. Not long ago, I pulled out the box in which they were neatly placed in chronological order. *Wasn't that just like my organized mother?*

The contents of these messages reflected mundane details of life as a soldier interspersed with numerous comments about the weather and how many days I had left before I got back home. I was careful to avoid matters of combat or the dangers of living in the jungle. But Mom knew. She tracked my unit as best she could and worried excessively, as mothers tend to do.

My correspondence contained many questions about what was going on in America. They reflected my political observations of a confused and changing America. I raised many questions but didn't get back any answers. *Why were people not supporting the President and the soldiers, for that matter?*

Things sure were different then. My letters questioned the anger and hostility that was prevalent throughout the United States. I observed that society seemed full of uptight and ill-informed people. I noted that Martin Luther King, Jr., and Bobby Kennedy, two notable civic leaders, had been murdered while I was in Vietnam. None of us grunts could believe what was happening, and political tensions among the soldiers were rising, though we were dealing with it.

My letters provide insights into my feelings about the American political turmoil and neighborly distrust. To me, people simply seemed to be mad at government. Unfortunately, much of the public took out their anger on those of us in the military. It made no difference whether a soldier was drafted or had enlisted. We were all duty-bound and ordered to serve and consequently felt the wrath of the ungrateful.

When I returned from Vietnam in 1968, protests were on the rise. They became increasingly more violent and much larger. But our government also had become less tolerant of dissent and more violent toward dissenters. I didn't like who we were becoming as a nation. We were supposed to be united through common beliefs that brought us together and bound us to one another in friendship and love.

I felt the treatment of protestors by the police during the Democratic Convention in Chicago was abhorrent and killing student protesters at Kent State callous and unthinkable. Surely, such government intervention was not legitimized by our soldiers' involvement in Vietnam. I became outraged at such behavior by our government and started to change my thinking about the correctness of our government leaders as they made decisions in a supposedly civil society.

I began to question authority. In my confused and hurt state of mind, I began the transition to the "wanting change" phase of my life. Interestingly, I began to have some compassion for those who disagreed with government decision-making in Washington, DC. I could see their point. If they were moral enough to flee to Canada and avoid the draft, and willing to accept the consequences of their actions—well, then so be it. I held no malice toward these individuals because my life experiences had taught me that life is more pleasant if we do not hold grudges and allow others to take responsibility for their own judgments about such complicated matters. I didn't always agree with these individuals, but they deserved to make their own choices. You gotta love the guarantees given us in the Bill of Rights.

I also figured out that living in a democratic society is not easy. In fact, it can be very complicated. The right path is not always easy or obvious. The best path for society is often a blend of the more obvious choices. But in America, we are afforded the freedom to follow any path we choose because it is individually guaranteed. Achieving consensus in decision-making in the civilian world is very problematic and challenging. We get to express ourselves and oppose any outside governments who would interrupt such expressions. I think that's the main reason American soldiers fight in wars in the first place.

Those turbulent times in our history eventually gave way to a more peaceful period. The people had forced the government to end the war and bring closure to that regrettable period, at least from a historical perspective. The memories for those who served or witnessed the unfolding of events, however, will not fade until future generations modify their approach to war and conflict. How about "Giving Peace a Chance?"

Those of us who lived in the 60s and 70s are forever affected by the social and political events that centered around the Vietnam War and the civil rights movement. It was certainly a difficult time for young people who were struggling to gain independence from parental influence and seek their own identity. Major disagreements had erupted between parents and their children over governmental decision-making. These arguments had gone from small household disagreements to national protests that continued for several years.

While young people today face some of these same challenges, their decisions are not encumbered by issues like free love, justice for all, or the military draft. Racism and a lack of trust in government decision-making still guide political discourse and remain prevalent. At least the discussions surrounding such issues appear to be more civil.

Some of us believe this social challenge is rooted in the activities that occurred during America's involvement in the War in Vietnam. Soldiers returning from Vietnam were essentially chastised by a public weary of war and who did not trust any statements made by our political leaders. Many returning veterans developed second thoughts about the justification for this nasty war. These hardened and battle-worn veterans soon added their voice to the national dialogue against the Vietnam War and demanded social change. These soldiers, through organizations like the Disabled American Veterans and the Veterans of Foreign Wars, petitioned Congress to treat the many disabilities derived from combat injury or exposure to agent orange. This part of the fight continues.

Fast forward thirty years to the time when Iraq and Afghanistan veterans started returning home. In contrast to the returning Vietnam vets, these soldiers were hailed as heroes and patriots. *What a difference a war makes!* Political leaders obviously had done a better job in developing trust with the public over these wars, and, of course, the draft has been eliminated.

Today, the public recognizes that soldiers are not the problem and, therefore, should not be the subjects of their political contempt. When duty calls, soldiers always respond and proudly do their job. They put themselves in harm's way so every American can enjoy the benefits of our Constitution and live in a free, though at times not very respectful, society.

Respect is a relative term as it does not seem to be apparent in everyday life since the end of the Great War. Sometimes soldiers die and should be honored. Their supreme sacrifice should be treasured. As a Vietnam veteran, I think Americans today are quicker to recognize the sacrifices made by the men and women of the military and the impact that separation has on their families.

It's about time! We are a better people because of it. One might say that Vietnam veterans finally get to hold their heads high because we now have a public that gives honor to our sacrifices.

I believe wars are failures in diplomacy and that soldiers are merely the ultimate enforcers of flawed government policies. The general public's political thinking about war and peace has evolved. As a public, we no longer disrespect our soldiers but rather recognize their essential contributions to a free society. Because of this new national attitude, the consensus is that those who served in Vietnam should also be thanked for their service.

This welcoming attitude means that we veterans can now show our "soldier pride" without fear of ridicule or disdain. This reconciliation means the decades-long chip on our shoulders can finally be removed.

I believe the sacrifices made by soldiers during the Vietnam era contributed to political change in our country by promoting a powerful dialogue about war and civil rights. The era of the Vietnam War was indeed a turbulent political time. While lacking in calm and civil discourse, it proved that extensive protests and political activism can affect change. This recognition, combined with "thank you for your service," helps the healing and the reconciliation that has been too long in the making.

Stated another way, these expressions of thanks *do* bring some closure to the bitterness we felt upon our re-introduction to society, even though it was a painful delay.

Chapter 35

My Pursuit of Happiness as a Civilian

The Army had given me a lot of responsibility and had fully trusted my ability to handle any situation and resolve any problem. I did things in Vietnam that could only be done by a nurse or a physician at home. I had no choice but to grow up fast. I learned from experience to trust my gut instincts and, for God's sake, "just make a decision!"

My service in Vietnam gave me a lifetime of experiences that have served me well. I have applied these hard-earned lessons to every major problem I've encountered since re-entering civilian life. My approach has always seemed to work. As a government lobbyist, I have used these techniques to help my clients negotiate the complexities of the political world.

I couldn't be a medical professional once I left the Army. I had tired of dealing with things beyond my control. I also figured I was not smart enough to become a doctor or a nurse. It was the science requirements, I think, that gave me heartburn. However, I did want to change the world. I used the GI Bill to finish my education, receiving a B.A. in political science from Mankato State College in 1972. After graduation, I set off to apply my "can do" attitude and got into politics and government.

After years of state government service, I formed a governmental affairs consulting firm in 1980. For the past five decades, I have been very active in politics and advocating for good public policy. I like to believe I've made Minnesota and the United States better places. My professional life is not nearly as exciting as my Vietnam experience, but it has been very rewarding. The confrontations are certainly different—and no one is shooting at me. I can handle this.

Upon graduation from college, I set out on a new mission to advance the quality of life for all citizens. I didn't want to work as an elected official, but I did want to work in the public sector and become involved in high-level public policy development. I joined the presidential campaign of Hubert H. Humphrey in 1972 and became responsible for coordinating the delegate operation in six states. In the end, the Democratic Party endorsed Senator McGovern for president, mostly because he was opposed to the war in Vietnam. Humphrey was also opposed to the war but remained silent for too long.

As vice president, Humphrey believed it would not be in the best interest of the country for him to oppose the president. His loyalty to President Johnson and his public support of the Johnson Policy on Vietnam eventually cost Humphrey the presidency. Humphrey's opposition to the war became well known when Johnson announced he would not seek another term as president. Unfortunately, the vice president was condemned by the public for the many missteps of Johnson. The public decided to trust Nixon and elected him president.

During the Humphrey campaign, I rubbed elbows with the powerful and elite in Washington, DC. I learned how to analyze complex problems of a different kind and, perhaps, even developed a few practical solutions of my own. The former vice president continued to teach me about empathy, integrity, honesty and the need to be a vigorous promoter of good ideas. He taught me the importance of advocating for people who do good work and making sure government decision-makers hear their voices. He called it "enfranchising the disenfranchised."

After that campaign, I accepted a job on the staff of Governor Wendell Anderson in Minnesota. I had a chance to apply the skills I'd developed in Vietnam, the knowledge I'd gained from a presidential campaign and Vice President Humphrey to help solve major problems confronting the citizens of Minnesota. I cherished the opportunity to apply my new personal system of critical thinking along with the power of developing solutions that would achieve the best impact for the citizens.

It didn't take me long, however, to realize that all the easy problems had been solved a long time ago and only the tough problems remained. I concluded it would take a lifetime of reflection and solution to keep us on the right democratic track.

Eventually, I became the deputy commissioner and for a short time commissioner of the Department of Administration for the State of Minnesota. I spent eight years in the department as a political appointee and served three different governors from both political parties. The job was much more about serving the needs of state government agencies and making good decisions on behalf of the citizens of Minnesota as opposed to promoting a political party agenda. It was a great experience, and I believe I served as a catalyst for the development of several good public policies.

My tenure in state government was very satisfying. It exposed me to new challenges and helped me further develop my skills. My techniques of problem analysis and risk assessment before executing a plan had been clearly shaped in combat. If I include patience and persistence, my method of making and executing better decisions is complete. I was very fortunate to learn the art of political management in a non-hostile environment. These building blocks continued to build my foundation of life and a fulfilling career. The foundation was laid in Vietnam, but the many blocks added along the way strengthened my resolve to make our country and state a better place.

I eventually left the executive branch and established my own public policy consulting firm. That's a fancy name for a lobbyist. I continued to remember my early lesson about how good people who do good things needed representation at the Minnesota legislature. I had found my new niche.

I learned that government affects the everyday lives of ordinary people. My goal was to energize businesses and non-profits to become engaged in the development of policies that directly affect them. Civic responsibility and public engagement are the hallmarks of our form of government. All wars throughout our nation's history, including Vietnam, adhered to the public purpose of protecting that right. From my point of view, if individuals and businesses remain silent, they will only become a victim of bad public policy.

Lobbyists, including civilian, non-professional lobbyists, empower people. By definition, it is the duty of lobbyists to educate politicians about the merits of their clients' causes. I believe lobbyists add value to democratic governance and improve the decision-making process. Lobbyists are the mechanics of the political/governmental decision-making process.

Representing organizations and individuals before legislative bodies is a noble and necessary profession. We lobbyists advocate, and we protect. We petition policymakers for a redress of grievances.

My wife, Kirsten, defines my profession this way: "Lobbyists are people you hire to protect you from the people you elected."

Until late, there were no lobbyists during the Vietnam War to represent the political interests of soldiers or their families. Perhaps that is why the war lasted so long!

Looking back, I'm pleased to have met the goals of civic engagement I had set for myself during my tour in Vietnam. I've been blessed with a professional life that has provided abundant personal satisfaction. I've also been blessed with a personal life that has given me more satisfaction than I probably deserve. While I believe I've made a difference in the world of politics, my professional roots were established in Vietnam.

Upon reflection, I think that I have played a small role in improving the quality of life for the public. While I refuse to accept blame for any bad decisions I made since 1967, I take credit for the good things government has accomplished FOR THE PEOPLE. And so it goes.

Chapter 36

WRITING MY STORY / Big Picture Legacy

This is why I am writing my story: I want family, friends and all citizens to more fully appreciate my everlasting desire to improve the quality of decision-making in our political leaders. It starts at the top of the leadership hierarchy in Washington, DC, and trickles down through all elected leaders and their approach to governance.

War is not just about the flag and imposing our self-determined value system on others. War is about the hardships endured by those who are sent to execute these policies. We should be able to expect that our leaders exercise sound judgment and fully commit to quality decisions because the bad decisions can kill a lot of people. The war didn't just impact the soldier; it had a profound effect on the families of the individual soldier as well. To my way of thinking, the burdens on our civilian leaders are simple. They must understand the overwhelming responsibility they have to truthfully justify their actions to our soldiers, their families and their communities. No need to justify decisions to God! Just us… "We the people."

History has documented the painful past and our political leaders' defective decision-making about the Vietnam War. I believe that when you reflect upon all aspects of the Vietnam War and its impact on our society, you must conclude that outstanding military tactics are insufficient to overcome a faulty strategy.

Well, Mr. President, if you think the price of war in human and financial capital is too high, then don't send troops in the first place! Fully informed public debate must occur before actions are imposed. The discussion must be civil, and the information used to justify positions must be honest and transparent.

I believe it is mandatory that our political leaders clearly articulate the rationale for putting soldiers in harm's way. Their reasoning can't be muddled or shrouded in mystery. Only then can such acts of conscience give meaning to the supreme sacrifices made by the 58,000 soldiers who died in Vietnam. In my mind, saying, "Communism is evil and must be stopped," failed to meet the test for sending troops to die in Vietnam.

I couldn't possibly share my story without reflecting upon important issues such as honor, integrity, duty, sacrifice and service to country. My feelings about such issues are woven into my story. I cannot possibly reflect upon my life as a soldier without recognizing the significance of such notions. I have witnessed brave men surrender their lives while taking these beliefs to their grave. So, I believe it is important for all Americans to cherish these values and recognize their relevance in a free society.

Every soldier thinks about these issues at one time or another. Essentially, we all recognize they are our country's founding principles and anchor America's value system. As combat soldiers, we came to the realization that we might have to lay down our lives for such noble considerations. If not for these principles, then for what?

I formed opinions on such matters during my tenure in the Army. Some of my opinions have softened and even changed. As I incorporate other views and political thinking into my perceptions, I seem to have a better understanding of who I am, or at least who I think I want to be. It took several years, but I have found inner peace through an evolution in my rationalization about the war and my experiences. I know and understand how danger and fear played havoc on my psyche, but I believe I was always true to my principles. Above all, I believe my actions in combat always reflected the morals of human decency.

I understand that politics, like war, is also a combat sport, and the participants should not be faint of heart. In the final analysis, however, adherence to democratic principles requires good analysis, transparency and honesty. These underpinnings will assure that integrity is the standard when dealing with the public on matters of consequence. Therefore, when it comes to making life-altering decisions, politicians must never dishonor our principles for the sake of political expediency.

At this station in my life, I believe we have learned from the mistakes of Vietnam and the harm that leadership decisions caused. I have no difficulty talking about the details of what it is like to be in combat because it provides a forum to discuss how soldiers get into combat in the first place and the everlasting impact of their experiences.

The members of the Big Red One fought and served our country proudly in WWI, WWII, Vietnam, Afghanistan, Iraq, and now the War on Terror. Our destiny does not end, nor do our individual stories. We owe it to the people who died in battle to tell their stories so that civilian leaders know the importance of making good decisions about war. Perhaps most importantly, the oath of enlistment into the military has no end point or limitation. We all took the oath to stand for freedom and defend liberty. Most of us still do that even though our fighting days are long past.

The Vietnam War has been written about extensively, and the decisions made by our political and military leaders have been thoroughly vetted for over five decades in the world of academia and by VFWs throughout the country. Even though the sacrifices made by the soldiers who served in Vietnam have not been forgotten, the debate goes on as to how best to change a system for making decisions that send soldiers to fight in such wars.

Has the history surrounding the Vietnam War repeated itself in the decades-long wars in Iraq and Afghanistan? Has our political leadership failed to learn from past mistakes? People of reasonable intelligence could surmise we are still fighting communism—but by a different name. Is it our job to undertake such global challenges in today's world?

And so the debate rages on. The complexity of the questions and answers about the Vietnam War and how it impacted so many families will always be a work in progress, and any useful conclusion will rely heavily on individual and societal perspectives.

I think my Vietnam combat experiences were not unique. That being said, it is not much of a stretch to believe the impact on thousands of other soldiers was similar to mine. Having lived through combat and having watched the ultimate withdrawal of our troops from Vietnam unfold on television, I am left sad and angry.

I have attempted to use my observations to provide better insight into my story. I have tried to provide a big picture so that my little picture has meaning. The United States became involved in the Vietnam Conflict shortly after WWII. Although 1955–1975 were the years of major political and economic involvement, the first American combat deaths occurred in 1959. I urge readers to reflect upon a few statistics I have found quite disturbing. These statistics make vivid the devastating impact on the lives and families of those who served in Vietnam.

- Total Killed in Action 58,319[2]

- Missing in Action 1,719

- Wounded in Action 303,635

- Combat medics KIA 1,247

- One out of every 11 Medal of Honor recipients was a medic.

- 61% of those who were killed were younger than 21 years old.

- The average age of a soldier in Vietnam was 19 years old.

---

2   Vietnam Helicopter Pilots Association 1993 Membership Directory, p. 130.

- The average infantryman in the South Pacific during World War II saw about 40 days of combat in four years. The average infantryman in Vietnam saw about 240 days of combat in one year, thanks to the mobility of the helicopter and the guerilla tactics employed by the North Vietnamese Army and the Viet Cong.

- One out of every 10 Americans who served in Vietnam was a casualty. Although the percent of total combatants who died in Vietnam is similar to other wars, amputations or other crippling wounds were 300 percent higher than in World War II. 75,000 Vietnam veterans are severely disabled.[3]

- MEDEVAC helicopters flew nearly 500,000 missions in Vietnam. Over 900,000 patients were airlifted (nearly half were American). The average time lapse between wounding to hospitalization was less than one hour. As a result, less than one percent of all wounded Americans who survived the first 24 hours, died.[4]

But the Vietnam War is not just about statistics. It is about all of us who are the survivors and how we have spent every day since the war reliving our experiences. It is also about our families and friends who gave us unconditional love upon our return. In most cases, they were the only ones.

But I digress. My story is about bravery, honor, valor and encouragement from the right folks at the right time, and unyielding understanding expressed by others when we did not understand ourselves.

When soldiers went to war in Vietnam, it was not a one, two, three or four-year commitment as our oath of allegiance to our Country

3   Army Battle Causalities and nonbattle deaths Statistical and Accounting Branch Office of the Adjutant General, June 1953.
4   Battle causalities comparison – History of the 1st Infantry Division Museum data base for Vietnam.

suggested. Many of us were part of the last American mandatory draft into military service. The draft required two years of mandatory service in the US Army. In January of 1973, as the Vietnam War was winding down, the Selective Service System announced there would be no further draft calls. We became an all voluntary military.

For me and many other veterans, it would be dishonest to say that the length of our service was calculated by the number of years we served in uniform. It would be more accurate to calculate all the years we spent reliving our experiences. For us, the war is etched into our brains, and the memories will never fade. Our battles will be fought and reflected upon until our last breaths. We challenge our minds to change the outcomes of events because we think about what could have been. Unfortunately, it is impossible to remove the heartaches.

These memories do not fade, and the sequel is always the same. We move forward in life because we must. I suspect this actuality is the common thread that binds all soldiers together and enables each of us to relate to one another no matter which war we fought or which branch of the military we served.

The Vietnam War left a lot of us wondering, "What the hell happened to our youth?" The war is about living with fear, overcoming our anxieties, and courage. In fact, most of us lived in fear the entire time we were in country. Perhaps that edge enabled us to survive.

For we survivors, it is about our heartaches and our nightmares. It is about executing tasks we never thought we could or would ever be challenged to perform. It is about the bonds we created with each other and the value of the "band of brothers."

War is about survival and dealing with the aftermath. The Vietnam War challenged the will of our country and our citizens' ability to endure. It was about the integrity of our leaders and the principles that guide our decision-making. It is about a soldier's ability to apply the life lessons learned in combat to everyday life.

In the final analysis, war was about putting aside the normal things of a teenager and rushing full-bore into adulthood where you had no choice but to learn how to cope with life's adversities. Many of us were drafted and sent to Vietnam to do our nation's bidding and engage in mortal combat, only to return to an ungrateful nation. What a terrible thing to do to young people.

Some Final Personal Thoughts

I think about my experiences in Vietnam every day. I think about who died and who was sentenced to a difficult life due to traumatic injuries and mental anguish. Since I left Vietnam, other than the death of my wife, parents and brother, I can truthfully say I have never dealt with anything that compares to the challenges of a grunt medic. Vietnam gave me a unique perspective and a special "can do" focus.

I didn't ask to go to war, but serving in the military was part of life back then. I paid attention, did my duty and survived. When I left Vietnam, I returned to my parents, who were still working and living in St. Paul, Minnesota. They were proud of me, but we didn't talk about the war or what I went through. I seemed to not have anything in common with family, friends or the public. The destroyed villages of Binh Doung Province had nothing in common with my old neighborhood on the East Side of St. Paul.

Unquestionably, I had transitioned from a boy to a man. I had proved my mettle and would never allow anyone to look down upon me or speak ill of my brothers. The early time home was stressful, and so time with my family passed very slowly. Normal conversations were problematic, so I appreciated that Mom and Dad gave me space. Soon enough, I began my new journey as a civilian and started to rejoin society. Finding peace and achieving some standard of normalcy was a challenge. Thank God, my parents were so supportive.

The first weeks back home, I remember riding a roller coaster of emotions. I couldn't relax, loud noises made me react in ways not common to civilians, and sleep did not come easily. I specifically remember being withdrawn and frustrated. I needed to get to my next duty station in Colorado because there, at least, I could handle the routine of blowing bugles, field exercises, dining with thousands, and being with lots of people in olive drab uniforms. I knew it would be much easier to relate to other soldiers who were returning from Vietnam. It still is.

I went to Fort Carson and unknowingly went through a version of combat detox. We were given slack by our superiors because they knew we would soon be discharged. We all still did our jobs, but not with the same level of enthusiasm and discipline as we exhibited in Vietnam. We sort of followed orders but in a more relaxed manner. As Vietnam returnees, we maintained the attitude of "what's the worst thing they could do to us? Send us to Vietnam?"

Nope, already been there and done that.

Getting my Honorable Discharge was a wonderful thing. I am proud of this accomplishment, and I have fully taken advantage of the benefits such recognition has afforded me. My first house was financed by the VA, my college education was paid for by the VA and all of my health care is provided by the VA. I deeply appreciate the fact that my service is recognized by my country and has led to something positive. Most importantly, my time at Fort Carson began the process of easing me back into the real world.

I did not contemplate my fate, nor did I fear it. Duty, honor, glory and love of country were common beliefs in my neighborhood when I was young. Getting drafted or enlisting was just a part of the natural evolution of becoming a good citizen and true to the male way of proving I was a man.

When I was a teenager, things were less confusing. We simply did what we were asked to do. We were cognizant of the military build-up in Vietnam, but it seemed so distant we didn't talk about it much. This was the era of President John Kennedy. We were ready to play our role in a society premised on, "Ask not what your country can do for you, but ask what you can do for your country."

Of course, in a few short years, our idealistic society attitudes would change. The mounting political pressure against the war would occupy everyone's attention and forever redefine us as a nation.

I remain honored to be a veteran and proud of this part of my life. In time, I was eventually certified as a disabled veteran by the VA. You know—the agent orange and PTSD thing. Some people say the war brought out the worst in all of us and was not worth the price we paid. But then again, being an optimist is part of the personality profile of a typical medic. I have consistently looked for the upside of every experience. I know good can emerge from some bad circumstances.

I took care of a lot of soldiers—at times, under extreme circumstances. From that perspective, I must believe the challenges I confronted and overcame were worth every moment. I boosted my confidence and my self-worth because of them. I did my job. In Vietnam, I learned how to navigate through the treacherous and distressing parts of life. In retrospect, Vietnam taught me that some of the routine duties in my life have been about managing inconsequential distractions.

Several years ago, when I was dealing with the death of my wife Donna, I was distressed because I couldn't fix her illness. To others, I probably came across as distant and emotionally uninvolved. I was sad for sure, and I felt helpless. I was simply coping with the circumstances and fortified my resolve by pushing forward as I did in combat. But just like the war, when it came to the really big things in life, I discovered you never quite reconcile the pain of loss.

Eventually, by example and activism, like-minded citizens changed the way politicians thought of war. Governmental decision-makers needed to be held more accountable for their actions. They needed to honest with the public.

If political healing and reconciliation are ever going to happen, we need to continue a civil discussion about the reasons we went to war in Vietnam. Unfortunately, it took the public at least thirty years to realize the crisis in Vietnam, and its political fallout was not the fault of the soldiers who fought it.

Would I do it all over again? Yes, I would, even if I knew the outcome would be the same. Maybe the best description I can share is: "I ended up being in the wrong place… but at the right time."

I believe that many of the values I cherish and the important lessons I learned while serving in the Army have made me a better person. I now realize that as a PEOPLE, we can change and adapt to new ways of thinking about our country. I am proud of my country and the hope for freedom that it symbolizes through political reform. Government decision-making and press transparency have evolved. Most importantly, I know that I am part of a very special group of people who answered the call and clearly understand the true meaning of being a patriot.

I conclude my story with the message contained in the last phrase of lyrics from the song, *I Will Never Be the Same Again* by Hillsong. These lyrics are from the inspirational preaching of Dr. Criswell. They have been slightly modified to appropriately fit my history and experience.

> I will never be the same again
> I can never return, I've closed the door.
> I have walked the path, I ran the race
> And I will never be the same again.

I still wonder what it would have been like to work in a hospital in Germany or Italy.

Postscript

*Greetings from the Mankato State
College Veterans Club
... now that's more like it*

I could not write about my experiences in Vietnam without talking about how this fish out of a war survived the political sea of unrest and discontent when I returned to a college campus. I was pissed off at the behavior of many students who we called "draft dodgers." Like most returning vets, I had a chip on my shoulder and only wanted to concentrate on school and avoid the havoc of social unrest for fear of doing something really stupid.

Like most returning veterans, besides being weary of conflict, I was withdrawn and escaped to the mental safety associated with being an introvert. It was a lonely life because I had nothing in common with the other students I met. Potential dating candidates asked me if I had "killed any babies." Such bullshit comments really hurt. It is still painful to rationalize such abhorrent behavior on the part of a few. *They could have just said "no" and left it at that!*

One day, while reading the student newspaper, I noticed an ad for a "Veterans Club Smoker." I had no idea what that was, but I suspected it would be worth going to the meeting since it was to be held at the local American Legion Club. Upon arriving, I quickly discovered the group was recruiting returning veterans to join this humble, but obviously proud, social organization. While there were only a dozen or so members in attendance, I immediately felt a strong bond of community and understanding. *What a pleasant surprise.* I knew I had found my collegiate safe harbor. Many of the compatriots I met that night would rapidly become life-long friends.

I regained my sanity and lasting inner peace through the Mankato State College Vets Club. We understood each other without delving into heavy personal reflections, although many of us did from time to time. We intuitively knew that having served our country set us apart from others on campus. As students, we were older, wiser to the world's mysteries, perhaps more reflective, and certainly not afraid of any challenges that professors could put forth.

This fine organization avoided the political protests of everyday life on a college campus in the early 1970s. Our Vets Club was a social organization primarily dedicated to the keg and was our reentry point to civilian life. Soon enough, the Club gained a reputation for being a safe harbor for our brothers and sisters who had just gotten out of the military. As members, we just wanted to have a good time and hang out with other veterans.

Our members formed a bond similar to that experienced in the brotherhood of military members. We helped each other with classwork, ran a roommate referral service and interacted with the college administration to resolve problems some vets had in getting their GI Bill benefits. We offered frequent opportunities to reflect upon the state of college affairs over cheap beer and cheap wine. It was wonderful!

The organization and command skills of our members made our monthly parties the pride of the campus. Our marketing philosophy of charging men five dollars while women got in free drew the biggest campus crowds to our parties. The former military police members of our club made sure no party attendees got out of control or became unruly. We also hired a local uniformed cop to help assure order. Our social events were well-organized and well-managed. We never had a security issue, and we made lots of money.

Consistent with the caring nature of our members, we shared our prosperity. We helped disabled veterans and provided support for community needs. We took care of any campus veteran who needed a helping hand or who needed a compassionate ear. In 1972, there were 1,100 veterans on our campus out of 14,000 students. Our Vets Club had more than two hundred members. Our spiritual needs were different from the younger college students. I'm sure every member suffered from what is now referred to PTSD.

As we had all learned in the service, no member was allowed to fail, and we made sure no vet gave in to their personal demons. To some, membership in the Vets Club was their salvation. Dealing with traumatic change and transition to civilian life was not easy back then. This organization and the special bonds we developed set the stage for each of us to enjoy a decent and good life after college.

Vets Club bonds remain strong and evident to this day. Several of us still get together every Saturday for breakfast and reflection. Where once we looked for the best beer establishments in town, we now look forward to our weekly serving of soft eggs or oatmeal and pancakes. More than a dozen pals participate in our weekly gatherings, so the therapy continues. Perhaps we are the longest running PTSD therapy group in existence.

Even though each of us has repeatedly shared the stories of our youth and college life after military service, they never seem to get old—*like all of us!*

Acknowledgements

There are two recent events that inspired me to write my story. They both occurred in the spring of 2017. First, I was asked by Buck McAlpin, a colleague and lobbyist, to be the luncheon speaker at the annual conference of the Minnesota Ambulance Association. Buck told me there would be about a hundred attendees. The Minnesota Ambulance Association is a fine organization deeply committed to advancing the profession of paramedics and EMTs and serving as a policy interface between the legislature and emergency responders. They hold educational seminars and recognize select members each year through their Stars of Life Award Program.

They met at a hotel near the State Capital because part of their mission was to lobby at the legislature that day on issues important to them. When I was first asked to be their luncheon speaker, I readily agreed because I have been a lobbyist for over forty years and was happy to share my professional and political insights with the group. Logical assumption, right? This assumption proved false—they did not want to hear my lobbying insights. I was somewhat taken aback when I was asked to share "what it was like to be a combat medic in Vietnam." I was told my audience would be people well-seasoned in providing lifesaving emergency care to the injured and curious about my experiences in rendering emergency care under combat situations. This group was familiar with the concept of PTSD and wanted to know how I learned to deal with the unpleasant side of life in a combat zone.

I agreed to share my recollections and began to put pen to paper. The subject material and my experiences were relatively easy to compile because many incidents are as fresh in my mind today as if they had occurred yesterday—not fifty years ago. As a professional government affairs specialist, I have given quite a few speeches over the years. It was an easy thing for me to do, and I have always enjoyed enlightening and empowering my audiences. This speech, however, was going to be different, and I knew it. It was the first time in five decades that I was formally asked to present my story. Old memories, some good and some bad, quickly came back to me. Because it was my story, I was intimately familiar with the subject matter. I knew it was important to be coherent and tactful while I addressed this weighty subject matter.

When the hour for my speech arrived, I was apprehensive. One sure thing was clear, though—butterflies are much easier to deal with than bullets. Pre-speech anxiety focused on: How would the audience react? Was I sharing too much detail? What kinds of questions would they ask? After a fine introduction from the host, I made my way to the podium and began sharing my saga. My voice remained calm and my cadence as steady as a soldier's march. At one point I became aware that all eyes were intensely focused on me. As the saying goes, "You could have heard a pin drop." But I pressed on. Twenty-five-minutes later, I received a standing ovation with shouts of "welcome home" and "thank you for your service." Their heartfelt expression brought tears to my eyes.

Shortly after, I used my professional skills as a lobbyist to help secure legislative funding for a public television initiative entitled Minnesota Remembers Vietnam. I was fortunate to work with Jim Pagliarini, the CEO of TPT, the local PBS affiliate, and Katie Carpenter, the Project Coordinator on this initiative. I testified before several legislative committees and shared my reasons for why this initiative would be significant to all Minnesota veterans. Our legislative efforts were successful and public television in Minnesota launched a yearlong campaign to highlight the impact of the Vietnam War on soldiers, families and society.

The goal was to capture and document these stories so they can forever be preserved and shared throughout our educational system. In addition, community outreach and local focus groups were held throughout the state. These community experiences brought a better understanding for many of those still suffering from profound yet unresolved issues. The project also included the creation of an internet-based "virtual story wall" that collects recollections that will serve future generations. The Wall That Heals, the Vietnam traveling Memorial, spent a few days in front of our State Capitol in Minnesota. The Wall That Heals and the events that surrounded it allowed everyone to appreciate the magnitude of the impact that the Vietnam War has had on our society. I was honored to be a part of this project.

Because of these two events, I decided to expand the reflections in my speech and legislative testimony, which ultimately proved to be a necessary therapeutic exercise. I now have a better understanding of some of the demons I have lived with all these years. As I began to reflect upon my role in the Vietnam War, I was reminded that the incidents that had occurred fifty years ago were as fresh in my mind as they were fifty years ago.

About the Author

Military Biography for (William) Bill Strusinski, aka "Doc"

Military Occupation Specialty (MOS): 91B (Combat Medic)

Primary Unit: HHC, 1 Bn/26 Inf, First Infantry Division - Most of my time was spent assigned to Company A, 1/26th

Highest rank achieved: Sergeant

Medals awarded:

- Combat Medical Badge
- Bronze Star for meritorious service – 9 September to 28 November 1967
- Bronze Star for Valor – 24 October 1967
- Bronze Star for Valor – 24 March 1968
- Bronze Star for Valor – 23 April 1968
- Army Commendation Medal – For meritorious service during the period August 1967 to July 1968
- Air medal – 7 September 1967 to 11 June 1968
- Good Conduct Medal
- Various unit campaign medals

Period of Service in Vietnam: August 1967 to August 1968

Made in the USA
Columbia, SC
18 October 2020